CTRM & ETRM Trading Software Strategies

Commodity & Energy Trading Software Strategies

Bruce Berley

Steven Berley

Antioch Book Publishing

ISBN: (ePub) 978-0-9882072-6-4

ISBN: (ePDF) 978-0-9882072-8-8

Contents

Acknowledgements.................................. 11

About The Authors 13

Introduction 15

Chapter 1: C/ETRM Evolution, not
Revolution 17

   Front-Office Systems History 19

   Risk Systems 23

   System Performance........................... 24

   Reports 24

   Back-Office Evolution 26

   Software Players 26

Chapter 2: C/ETRM Current State:
Mature? 29

   CTRM/ETRM Systems.......................... 32

   Scheduling or Logistics Systems: 35

   Bid/Award and/or Price Posting Systems 37

   Physical Optimization, Big Data or Risk
   Systems 38

   Market Pricing Systems 40

   Credit Systems.................................. 40

Accounting Systems............................42

Spreadsheets & Add-ins 43

Business Intelligence (BI).....................45

Chapter 3: C/ETRM Future State.............47

One Size Finally Fits All 47

Too Many Players 47

Consolidation 51

Big Software Players............................53

Standardized Software Platforms...........57

The Ultimate Future State 58

Chapter 4: Industry Talent....................61

Chapter 5: Big Data 65

Chapter 6: Valuation Models..................73

Black Holes vs. Black-Scholes 73

Chapter 7: Cloud and SaaS 79

Chapter 8: Selecting Consulting Firms......85

What's the Real Game Being Played?.....85

Consulting Firm Intercept or Disruption? 88

Chapter 9: Transactional & Referential Data 95

Referential Data 97

Transactional Data............................. 99

Chapter 10: Project Scoping: Everything is
in Scope.. 101

Process Reviews 102

Chapter 11: Defining Requirements: The
Behavioral Science and All of Those "A"
Words 107

AAA.. 107

Requirements Examples 118

Chapter 12: Software Vendor Selection: The
Art and Science of Momentum 122

Software Demonstrations – The Demo. 126

Proof of Concept............................... 128

Proof of Concept Purchase 130

Free Trials 132

The Software Sells Itself.................... 133

Software Vendor Roadmaps............... 134

Patches, Releases & Upgrades 135

Chapter 13: Front-2-Back Software
Assessment Ideas 138

Front-Office Capability 139

Has your software company's CEO read Mr. Berley's book, *Energy Trading and Risk Management*, especially the end? 140

Will you show me how many front-office reports you have? Great, please open them. 140

How many, and which, reports do your other clients use out-of-the-box? 141

Can I get real-time position reports? Yes, you can. 142

What valuation tools are embedded into the system? 143

Trade capture 144

Book structure and price indexes 146

System performance 147

Middle-Office Capability 149

Risk 149

Middle-office daily control reporting .. 150

Scheduling 150

Credit 151

Back-Office Capability 152

Chart of accounts 154

Settlement................................... 154

Tax 156

FASB/IFRS reporting...................... 156

Regulatory reporting...................... 157

Inventory 158

Contracts..................................... 160

IT department.............................. 161

User guides.................................. 162

Offshoring extensions 163

Summary...................................... 165

Chapter 14: Project Planning: More Art than Science 168

Chapter 15: Project Execution: *Basics* is the Name of this Game........................... 177

1. Establish psychological safety 178

Alternative organizational behavior approach 179

2. Cleanse the software vendor's database 182

3. Get your data ready before project kick-off................................. 185

    Referential data............................ 185

    Transaction data........................... 188

4. Bring design consultants into the project 190

    Are we ready for the implementation consultants now?........................... 190

5. Develop and test designs and extensions 192

6. Train users.................................... 196

7. Perform User Acceptance Testing (UAT) 198

8. Go live.. 201

Chapter 16: Post Project Assessment: Benefit Analysis 205

Chapter 17: Upgrading your C/ETRM System 209

Chapter 18: Switching ETRM Systems 211

Chapter 19: Key C/ETRM Success Factors.. 213

Acknowledgements

We wish to thank Antioch Book Publishing for providing me the avenue to write this book. Thank you for allowing me, once again, to utilize your ability to deliver with great care for society.

We would like to thank the untold software vendors who provided some clarity on avenues I was less familiar with. Your input is clearly in this book and available for future clients. They will now have better information, to independently move toward finding your software as an option as well.

And, to our family for supporting us every step of the way to enjoy this adventure without hesitation.

About The Authors

Bruce Berley

Mr. Bruce Berley is a 25-year expert trader, and software expert, trading in metals, agriculture, metals, and currency. Bruce has been instrumental in developing both fundamental and technical trading strategies. In the software arena, Bruce developed proprietary, complex commodity and energy retail pricing software that validated volume and settlement data.

Bruce possesses an MA in computer science from Wright State University and BS from Colorado College.

Steven Berley

Steven Berley has a BBA in Finance, an MBA, and is a CPA. He has authored several articles on topics from energy to enterprise risk management strategies, from cover stories to editorials, in a variety of magazines and outlets, including his book, *Energy Trading and Risk Management.*

Starting his career in energy just after graduate school in 1994, Mr. Berley entered directly onto the 30th floor – "the trading floor" – for one of the most infamous trading scandals, save the 2008 financial crisis. His incredible curiosity and passion for understanding and applying trading concepts in economic ways has lead Mr. Berley on an incredibly rare path of working as a controller, risk director and trading leader; or, as we say in trading, in every role, front, mid and back. He has worked at Enron, Koch Supply & Trading, and Shell. Mr. Berley successfully traded profitably in all of his five consecutive years.

Introduction

Steven's first book, *Energy Trading and Risk Management,* was deliberately published before this one to ensure that the practitioner first considers and understands the implications of their trading and risk management programs before buying, upgrading, or replacing their software with what appears, on the surface to be the *best* software.

The one thing you will take from this book is independence. I will provide ideas and alternatives that may, at times, appear to contradict using my service or any other third party consulting firm. For example, I will suggest software packages that may only take 3-6 months to implement over ones that other firms are lining up for 18-36 months of billing. It might seem counter-productive for me to recommend a shorter project, but my goal is to recommend what you actually need, not what will actually pay us more.

Although we wrote this book without influence, we did get input from multiple industry players, from consumers to CEO's, in software, and from consulting and client arenas alike.

Before moving into purchasing or upgrading your software, you will have to spend a tremendous amount of time assessing and reviewing vendors. Not just for functionality, but, more importantly, for the project culture in your company, the consulting firms, and the software vendors in relation to your business.

For more information of how **Front-2-Back** Consulting can serve you, and for some bonus information and downloads, visit: www.frontmidback.com/book-bonus

Chapter 1: C/ETRM Evolution, not Revolution

The key to this evolution, not revolution, is that most people in business, who have never worked in commodity or energy trading, quickly learn that this space is a paradox.

Trading operates at twenty times the pace than any other company activity, yet it moves slowly in time in comparison to the other technological advances we are now all accustomed to.

How and why does paradox this exist?

If you work in trading, you understand that each and every day, not at month-end, a profit and loss statement is generated, along with untold trading, risk and accounting reports. This makes commodity and energy trading run about 20 times faster than traditional business operations.

Which means that there is no time to stop, discern, evaluate, provide feedback, buy, and implement trading software. Developers can't keep pace with the trading business. Often times, software is developed client-by-client, which means that any C/ETRM, or Risk system is far from standardized.

Add in that traders – I have been one too – often throw stuff over the wall to the mid- and back-office to discern. They then say the middle and back-office are not keeping pace with the change of our trading and hedging programs. Of course, they are not. Having spent time working in back-, mid- and front-office roles, I can appreciate the other side of the wall much more! Stopping, and saying "thank you" will be the humbling experience once you have lived each every role, front-to-back.

If you haven't worked both sides of the fence, by reading this book you will learn why and how software systems are sold to you, and who is the beneficiary of these systems. That will be an irony in itself, but will explain one of many reasons why projects take longer, require more money, and are usually not as successful as expected – i.e. the benefits one can leverage can be uncovered throughout the project, real and perceived.

In getting to the real benefits of commodity and energy trading systems, to bring them full circle from the 20th century into the 21st century, we will spend a brief time on this evolution – the history of these systems – for perspective.

I realize what is important is where are we today, and where are going in the CTRM/ETRM space. History repeats itself though, and it is important to know when, where, why and how your current or prospective CTRM/ETRM firm is headed.

Front-Office Systems History

Since the front makes the money, it is still it is the focal point for how and why trading and risk management software systems are developed and sold to clients. Understanding trading portfolios, exposure reporting, and capturing deals is the underlying essence these initial systems brought in the 20th century, and still bring today, to hang their hat on.

After this book, though, your perspective may begin to change.

When these systems were first introduced, they were certainly more physical-transaction based, with deal capture and some basic logistics process steps, to appear like an energy trading and marketing software niche. Many of us new to software in the 1990's, especially when it really became a big industry, focused on this one front-office feature in search of how it could take a transaction as far into our processes as possible before it had to get extracted – not interfaced, but extracted – and re-keyed so we could continue the customer-to-cash process. It still happens today, but for the wrong reasons.

At this initial stage, the software provided one main feature and that was to ensure the trade was captured. When you worked at Enron, or

Koch, or Shell, hand-written tickets were coming in the mid- and back-office in piles, including when the traders were leaving at 5:30 or 6:00pm. Which meant the mid-office had to work for several more hours, with many working not just 12 or 15 hours a day. I had one guy who worked 17.5 hours every day, including weekends. Lance was a hero, and he was treated and respected as one, but he, too, burned out and moved on to bigger and better things.

Just trying to get a trader to enter a trade into these new systems was painful. Today it is expected, and even measured as a part of many traders' bonus programs. We have come a long way in building expectations and accountability, but is it enough?

For logistics too, it was a start for tracking a physical deal, but as all schedulers experience today, they, too, are a niche group and their software, as we will discuss, is still immature and lacking.

In looking for systems that could take a transaction, in a complete state, as far as it could, which was about to the middle-office for a basic position report, we all realized we needed to ask for reports, that did not come with the system. Not a lot has changed here either.

Reporting was an after-thought, as it usually is in most projects, even today. Big hint.

The reports would serve others who were keying the deal information into other systems. Other systems being multiple, from scheduling to settlement, to accounting, to contracting. Financial reporting, as you can see, was a non-existent thought in those days.

However, since we were running trading books on DOS – yes DOS – the systems could not handle as much data as they can today.

Thirty thousand rows running on these systems was big data then. And, our desktops had memory not measured in GB or MB, but in KB. Even my Sun Microsystem supercomputer desktop was in KBs. Therefore, any data size was not nearly what they are today, so calculations could take all night to run. I know we have similar problems today, but data size is now much greater, and growing by the day.

Risk Systems

When I say risk back in the day, I mean the ability to calculate a deterministic Value-at-Risk, or VAR. That was usually done through home-grown systems or spreadsheets with one simple, deterministic value published. Yes, we also did it on post-it notes.

Scenarios, and/or simulations then, were rarely performed, save the times I ran untold iterations by changing the price, volatility and correlation curves/matrices in each step in either DOS or Spreadsheets, or in the new ETRM systems. One-off calculations done on the side is the best way to describe those times. Hit the "calc" button, or F9, and go to lunch, the gym, or home, and return at 6am to see the results.

Many are asking what the difference is today in these commodity and energy trading systems? For most of these systems, save a few, we will discuss why you still have the same issue of running scenarios today.

System Performance

LOL – based on what you have already heard, it was an issue then, just as it is today, and will be tomorrow, for sure. Once this is solved, it will propel the next generation of commodity and energy trading system companies. Options are usually the culprit, modeling assets as options, that is, even using deterministic models, really slows calculation times.

Reports

I have mentioned this briefly above, ensuring I mention it again, and I will mention in about twenty-five more times in this book. It took me a decade to really internalize this is a key factor in all facets of the system life cycle.

I worked on not only some of the first ETRM systems, but also on some of the first accounting system implementations with software firms who were purchased – D&B had an accounting system which was very competitive and quickly purchased – or still exist today, that were in the same immature state. One of the key things I learned early on was from a project manager who said, "The first thing we have to do before we do anything, is to start this project by defining the reports."

Defining them by discerning every last data input, and how it must be designed, to meet those reporting needs.

Said another way, why does every company have a data repository?

Reports that were not thought of, changing market conditions, and especially not having thought through the reporting needs and then backing those needs into the very specific data attributes.

Today, I still have yet to see someone make the suggestion at the beginning of a project as I did on my first software project. A few have, though, and I will make an example of that later to bring history to full circle, to ensure you develop a great process and a great project outcome.

Back-Office Evolution

There was nothing. I assume you expected to hear this. Nothing designed for the back-office, not even an invoice just twenty years ago. Today there are systems that still produce nothing more than invoices. There are others that have all sorts of functionality to leverage.

Software Players

In this book, I will not use any software vendor or consulting firm names. The reason is that any use of any software firm impedes my, and our, independence in providing service to the industry. To suggest one firm over the other, or to even mention a firm can create perceptions that I may not intend to create.

I will state that I have worked to help some, over others, develop their first modules, including bringing them into new products. For example, when a firm tried to sell me a physical natural gas system while working in crude oil in both physical and financial derivatives, they had to modify and create new modules. They did it well, and timely.

As a controller, I had a summer intern, a junior from Texas A&M, running the mid-office oil derivative book; that is how good that system was developed and easy to work with. We hooked, just as many do today, one of the major option valuation tools, old-school black-scholes. If you read Steven' Trading and Risk Management Strategies books, these models are an issue.

Today, there are still systems that I could not teach a college intern to run over the summer. Between evolving and being more user-friendly than others, though, there are better choices to consider, now, than ever before.

The key point is that I have seen how and why one of the key players, who was sold at least twice in the last five years, was much more successful than others who had started twenty years ago. I witnessed, first-hand, directly to the top, how they operated their companies as compared to others. I, therefore, know what it takes to make them successful. I have also seen the laggards who just hang on.

In knowing this, I will convey why it is important to look not at the number of years a software vendor has been in business, but where they are now, and especially where they are headed. Therefore, the players who started this industry are important in moving the industry forward. Where we go from here will be key.

For more information of how **Front-2-Back** Consulting can serve you, and for some bonus information and downloads, visit: www.frontmidback.com/book-bonus

Chapter 2: C/ETRM Current State: Mature?

Fast forward to 2016. We have come a long way in 20 years, yet the CTRM/ETRM space has not matured, front-2-back. That is a great thing, as there is still tremendous opportunity for a select few software firms to realize explosive growth in the next decade.

We need to explore these implications further, as we develop the selection process, especially in scoping and defining the *must-have* and *nice-to-have* requirements. As we seek to ensure expectations through to implementation, we need to consider which option provides the solution that benefits you and meets your company's objectives, start to finish.

One of the key developments in the last few years is that we no longer think in terms of either ETRM *or* CTRM systems. Those that were solely ETRM systems are now venturing into the CTRM space and vice versa. They are now C/ETRM systems, which is critical.

Risk systems, settlement systems, and logistic systems are also branching out to becoming complete customer-to-cash solutions. Some by design, and some by customer modification.

We need to therefore establish what is a traditional CTRM/ETRM system by classes of software usage, not vendors. Some of these are full transaction systems and some are specialized tools. Some of these bolt-on to one another via interfaces developed at the client level.

There are a few instances where a vendor has a pre-developed interfaces with pricing or logistics systems, but those still need additional coding work at implementation. Accepting that a vendor has some pre-developed interfaces, though, may be riskier than buying one without pre-developed interfaces as they may actually provide the functionality you need. Why confirm this suggestion? Someone is selling you something they have developed that they know does not meet your needs, but may meet 65% of your needs, which isn't half bad in this space.

Before moving forward, I will define the commodity and energy systems into classes or buckets. The order does not indicate quality, nor does it suggest the order in which you should decide to buy these systems. I have also separated two classes due to the continued, non-standard way they are used in the commodity and energy markets – accounting and credit.

1. CTRM/ETRM Systems
2. Scheduling or Logistics Systems
3. Bid/Award and/or Price Posting Systems
4. Physical Optimization, Big Data or Risk Systems
5. Market Pricing Systems
6. Credit Systems
7. Accounting Systems
8. Spreadsheets & Add-ins
9. BI – Business Intelligence Systems

CTRM/ETRM Systems

CTRM/ETRM systems are generally defined as transaction capture systems to processing a trade from customer to cash. They are clearly much more developed with the front-, mid- and back-office needs in mind. They are growing in capability every year. However, where they are, or where they should be, is still not at the level of maturity most expect.

Today, prospective clients are asking, and assuming, we have passed the stage of having several basic transaction steps and valuation techniques, and that these systems are not just in the cloud, but have hand-held apps to capture trades, up to providing reports via your smart phones.

Slow down...

The current state has developed to include processes from modeling assets as options, to contract management, valuation, reporting, credit, scheduling, settlement and accounting, including regulatory reporting. A front-, mid- and back-office transaction capability.

However, the state of this front-2-back process and transaction capability is still basic, and not fully developed for more generally accepted sophisticated requirements. There are a myriad of reasons I can suggest to sound like an expert, such as: markets and instruments are constantly changing, new markets are moving into these systems, and especially where the power of valuation to managing big data has surfaced a critical need in the last few years.

Standardization is still not what any two companies would expect, much less an entire industry. What is sophistication one company won't entertain buying, is a must-have for others. Some are getting behind, some have gone the wrong direction, and some are moving rapidly forward.

Which direction are you moving?

Why?

There is this unwritten rule in the CTRM/ETRM space – when a client says, "That is industry standard, why don't you have that?" you learn very quickly to acknowledge and move on to the next point. If you have worked in the C/ETRM space directly, you are cringing that I've even mentioned this little issue. If you are on the trading side, you have an expectation; and that expectation is fair.

We will explore the contradiction in expectations, human nature, and reality as we move forward in the selection process. Just know, for now, it is there. Expectations and perceptions will cross into the human nature issues I previously discussed in *Energy Trading and Risk Management*.

To be a true expert, understanding and preparing yourself for this human nature is going to make the system, scoping to implementation, much easier.

If I were to summarize the current state of CTRM/ETRM systems, it is generally one of deterministic outcomes, without simulation capability, though many claim it is there.

Real-time positions and profitability are generally not there, or are half-baked. Scheduling is still basic and lacking in many avenues. Accounting components are evolving, but due to unique needs, beyond what most may expect, from balance sheet reporting, to regulatory requirements and income recognition, to hedge accounting, you have to open the hood and really see what is wired and what is missing. Though we now have evolved from the front-office all the way through to the back-office, or from customer to cash, CTRM/ETRM systems are still very basic in nature for all roles involved. Do not be discouraged though. There is power in leveraging data integrity across an entire front-2-back process: cost advantages and controls you can leverage sooner than later, adding the necessary, more sophisticated tools later – or simultaneously, for the willing.

Scheduling or Logistics Systems:

Moving product from trains to transmission lines, or ships to solar. These systems are generally the bolt-on systems needed today by most CTRM/ETRM users. There are niche markets within this logistics segment by product, especially within power. Many companies actually take the CTRM/ETRM transactions off into these systems via interface, to move product and then bring the transaction back into the CTRM/ETRM system for settlement and then into accounting.

A few companies may just use one of these systems instead of an entire C/ETRM system. One of the key issues is that markets are all so different. In looking just at power, there are so many different rules and processes of moving power in the U.S. alone, much less around the world. It is daunting even for these niche software players to keep up. No doubt, even in using these niche systems, local client development is needed to not only interface with other systems, but to provide the local norms and rules in data flow to ensure a complete transaction. The next class, too, has overlap within this class from shadow settlement to actually settling out of some of these systems.

Bid/Award and/or Price Posting Systems

These systems are specifically used for particular products and markets, for transmission to plant delivery into the marketplace. Whether natural gas or power, system bulletin boards for bid/award postings are geared solely toward a niche within a niche. There is an overlap, here, with the scheduling/logistics systems as some of the bolt-on systems do have a portion of this capability. With one system doing one part of the transaction and another system doing something different. For example, in power, one system may be good for the bid/award process, while the other is better at the shadow pricing/settlement/valuation process.

When I discuss where we are going in the future with all of these system classes, this will be an interesting facet to see how it develops.

Physical Optimization, Big Data or Risk Systems

As I define this arena, I am sure a few will debate that I've lumped these together, but it is not terribly relevant. The keys are both the amount of data and the sophistication of calculations provided. These systems focus on pricing deals, forward out decades, to managing real-time physical flow and pricing of products. I'm getting ahead of myself, this is the future. Or, is it?

Today, these systems are still seen as a PhD-level need, but recently, many companies have realized in their CTRM/ETRM implementations, that those systems do not provide what these tools provide in spades. This is one of the areas where expectations and perception of what was purchased and delivered cross paths often in projects today.

Everyone from traders to leaders now expect to see hundreds of thousands of simulations using regression analysis, AR1, Brownian Motion, and fundamental and financial market products, with their prices and respective correlating inputs, and volatility, running optimal pricing and transportation solutions.

When I say financial, I am talking volatility and correlation analysis, not just deterministic inputs, as in most CTRM/ETRM systems, for calculating a singular outcome. I am also saying fundamental factors – such as more granular level plant costing and capacity factors, including correlating factors such as weather, or supply, demand factors, which are crucial, to most users in our space.

These tools are starting to bring the power of both economics and mathematics into one arena, including consumer dynamics. I no longer see them as just PhD tools, but rather as must-haves in many markets, to truly understand everything from planning to trading. Where this class of systems is headed is another interesting perspective, but I will share my thoughts on this later. Today, I have seen a few companies who have purchased CTRM/ETRM systems when what they really needed was this class of software.

How does this happen? It comes down to who has the best sales staff.

Market Pricing Systems

All I am referring to here, is how the market prices are received or retrieved and inserted into your valuations and kept for historical reference. My point in mentioning these is simply that some CTRM/ETRM firms are building interfaces with these systems – Bloomberg-like systems. I will add, too, that many have interfaces mostly baked into the CTRM/ETRM systems for capturing exchange trades. A must-have in an active trading shop.

Credit Systems

Though many CTRM/ETRM systems come with credit modules, it is very, very common that a company will buy this specific module from a credit vendor or a major CTRM/ETRM firm. Standardization just seems non-existent in this space.

Approaches vary widely by company in this arena. I have been around for plenty of credit events. When I traded, Enron owed my trading book $2.4 million dollars, and there was no software predicting that quick downfall. Credit events usually happen quickly. For some, it is clearly a discernable downfall that one should limit their exposure to. Due to this non-standard arena, from functionality to performance, the credit arena will have to bring solutions, not just expect the software vendors to have a solution prepared for dozens, if not hundreds, of credit processes and valuation needs.

Its current state is, therefore, more in limbo and having a hard time finding direction for standardizing and satisfying every client. This means discerning the product before you buy is critical here. There are plenty of stories where companies, in recent years, have switched from one credit system to another, only to be disappointed.

Accounting Systems

When I discuss accounting systems, I am not talking about Microsoft Dynamics or Oracle Financials, I am talking about the accounting capability embedded into CTRM/ETRM systems. I carve this out especially for the accounting, back-office groups to truly understand.

The spectrum of expectations and perceptions in this area has been, and still is, challenging. And that's putting it nicely. The benefits, though, could be tremendous. These varying degrees of human nature are due to the perception, real or sold, that CTRM/ETRM systems can fully provide one's accounting needs. In nearly every case, it does not. Dissatisfaction occurs often. Whether it is the level of detail in accounting ledgers and subledgers, the reporting capabilities, hedge accounting, or FASB/IFRS pronouncements, much less the basic short term and long term asset and liability bifurcation, these systems often do not live up to expectations. In many cases, you should be prepared for material modification. Don't despair; I see major potential here, and one way or another, change is coming, especially if you hire us to help you scope and select systems, front-2-back.

Oftentimes too, accounting is not within the scope of the project, and I have had to highly suggest accounting needs to be established now, not in six months. In the future state, I will spell out what is important to discern in selecting software and setting expectations so that perceptions, or misunderstood human nature, is minimized for you and your company, and you can unpack the <u>many</u> benefits accounting systems can deliver.

Spreadsheets & Add-ins

If you use spreadsheet add-ins for running valuations for simulations, your add-ins will quickly become obsolete. In using add-ins, one risks short-term "busts," and systems that aren't capable of handling big data. Your system will become outdated quickly, in that I see those using add-ins struggling more and more, playing to catch-up every year.

As I mentioned in my first book, I am a big fan of Koch Industries, not just because I worked there, but for the leadership story I shared in *Energy Trading and Risk Management*. My point about Koch is that they do not spend money on things that do not prove a return on investment.

When I worked at Koch, we were growing rapidly and hiring lots of people. We needed new computers for the new staff and an executive asked me, "How is that computer you are buying going to make me money?" I have to admit, at 31 years old, I was a little dumbfounded. I quickly realized, though, he wasn't being old-school. He was giving me a perspective to help think in economic terms, terms where everyone must contribute to profits.

Another time, executives questioned when and how the new company-wide accounting system was going to exceed the amount spent to send a man to the moon. Seriously, the question came up and it was fair.

My point is that Koch was spending money on CTRM/ETRM systems, including building in-house systems, back in the 1990's and paving the way for a few firms to grow their products through our requirements and through co-development. Today, Koch is over ten-times larger than it was at that time. What I am saying is that you have to invest in systems to get their benefits to leverage your growth too.

Business Intelligence (BI)

If you don't have one, get one, now! This circles back to reporting. No system, in any class above, can provide the reporting to meet everyone's needs. You can certainly make custom reports in many of these systems, but the more you request reports, the more money you spend, which will often exceed the cost of a BI tool, but still not meeting reporting needs for today, or for the future.

Many of the systems above do sell the "drill" capability, but that doesn't mean the system can provide the reports you need. Drilling is more of a deterministic, fixed approach to certain data columns and a combination of data tables. Therefore, never take the bait that "slicing and dicing" is a replacement for having a BI tool that can pull data from any column or table in a manner you want and need.

For more information of how **Front-2-Back** Consulting can serve you, and for some bonus information and downloads, visit:
www.frontmidback.com/book-bonus

Chapter 3: C/ETRM Future State

One Size Finally Fits All

Although a one-size-fits-all solution isn't likely, I can certainly promise we will get to a better, more integrated state. How and why we will get there, though, won't simply be organic. Industry changes are coming, in my view. The implications of that will be higher, not lower price tags, but you will get what you pay for.

Too Many Players

Today there are currently too many players in this space. Why? Because firms build the system and sell it for great profits to the highest bidding private equity firm. It is no secret that a few software vendors have fetched nearly $1 billion on a fraction of revenue. Their EBITDA multiples have been rather large – I'm not talking 5-7 EBITDA, but more like EBITDA multipliers in the teens.

Combine the CTRM and ETRM spaces into C/ETRM, and we have a space race. The space to occupy the leadership board, sell, and move onward is no doubt on many software vendors' minds. We are all wondering who will be around and who won't.

I will, however, make a public bet that we will not have so many different software classes, or bolt-on software products ten years from now. That is almost a certainty. Expectations and rapidly changing markets will force horizontal integration, without fail.

It's both the vertical and horizontal integration that is likely the great debate. Outsiders consolidating this space is a possibility I will save for the end of this chapter.

In the interim, there are too many CTRM and ETRM firms cross-pollinating each other's space. Weak commodity prices are not the reason for it, nor will it make any difference, because we simply have too many firms.

Therefore, expect consolidation to begin sooner than later. Expect that an up-and-comer will evaporate, as will at least one, if not two, old-school players literally succumb, then sell.

If your software is one that is consolidated into a larger company, is that good for you? It could be. And, it could be your software versions are about to become obsolete, and discontinued.

On the other side, expect another up-and-comer to rise to the top.

As I said in the beginning, I am not divulging who, and certainly not why in this book. I have a formula, though, of what has been successful in this industry, who is developing what, why, and the differentiation between these firms – which at times appears subtle but at others, more obvious.

As for horizontal integration, the project expectations have not been met with a supposed one-size-fits-all approach. Untold, brilliant clients have attempted this approach. It does not work.

At least two, if not four or five of the software system classes I mentioned above, are needed to bring a commodity or energy trading and risk management system project to fruition with both basic tools and basic reporting, but also with all of the physical and financial needs, sophisticated valuations, logistics, and accounting aspects on the table.

Markets are too volatile, and with untold vendors and untold consulting firms running around suggesting this system and blocking that up-and-comer, a breakthrough is inevitable and trust is a big issue in this industry today. Period, end of story. Trust is an issue.

In public, I wouldn't be so forthright, but in a book that you are reading, we are simply having an eye-to-eye conversation. For many, we will have that conversation directly as well.

Why, then, is consolidation taking longer than one would expect? Traders are not the only A-type, oftentimes AAA-type, running in our markets. Smarter-than, better-than, and get-out-of-my-way attitudes are ever present in the software space, like no other too.

There is a difference, though, between tenacity and winning.

Issues in consolidating the C/ETRM space stem from some of the issues I point to, especially, in the last chapter of my last book, *Energy Trading and Risk Management*. The trading strategies, so to speak, of certain software vendors, in trading lingo is 'long' and 'short' the opposite of what the best trading strategy of all time has produced!

Consolidation

Consolidation, though, may happen through organic development. Certain firms recognize the trajectory and are adjusting. They may become self-made, although some already claim that today, and the rest of the story will play out in the coming years.

As this one unfolds, there is speculation that outside influences are noticing the valuation this commodity and energy software space has brought onto itself in the last few years.

There are thoughts, too, that big software firms see the commodity and energy space as nothing more than additional transactions to process, not real differentiation. This means they either start buying up firms or they claim they can do commodity and energy trading and risk management because it all tastes the same – like chicken.

Unfortunately, chicken can be prepared in a variety of ways, and if they don't have that canary checked for bird-flu, someone is going to get more than an upset stomach. I understand the thought that a trade is nothing but a transaction – it is. But what I am not sold on is that big software vendors, without buying the right flock, will be able to deliver any better than the rest. Especially if they send in non-trading experts.

That is where the issues are today – knowledge about trading. This industry is not short, but really, short trading and risk knowledge in all facets.

Big Software Players

Beware, they are coming for this space. How they do it may be surprising. By buying C/ETRM firms, or by developing the capability in-house? Both.

Their approach does make sense in that many of these players are going to existing clients and selling the solution as an add-in component or suite of commodity and energy trading capabilities, from front-2-back. This is logical and probably some quick, easy wins that they leveraged from existing clients. Clients have already paid hundreds of millions, to well into the billions. I know, I have worked in a variety of capacities in accounting projects from $30 million to $1.6 billion.

For clarity, these big software players do not sell C/ETRM price point projects. Their business models have been to sell to large corporations who can pay the billion-dollar price tags. This means they did not walk into an existing client and offer a $2-5 million-dollar C/ETRM-like software products. They charge much more, and they know with certainty they cannot just show up into the traditional C/ETRM space and offer these immaterial sized projects, as they see them.

No doubt, they have a long horizon to leverage their current client base to build, or rather have them pay for, their R&D for the C/ETRM system capability. A good move.

Buying a C/ETRM vendor and folding it into their big software generally seems, to me, to be a better approach. Because the EBITDA multiples of the past, they continue to build, rather than buy. Somewhere, consolidation prices will balance.

Why and how do I provide this suggestion?

I have hinted, and will speak further, to the talent in the commodity and energy space. I have been in the commodity and energy trading arena for a long time and I see really smart college graduates showing up with 3.9 GPA's from well-known colleges. I have discussed with many how long it takes for someone to get up to speed to be effective in working on software engagements.

I know how long it takes for someone who is hired straight out of college to work in a narrowly-defined area of trading, say for the mid-office. Based on that input, and my experience, professionals take three years, and many often take more than that to really digest energy trading in their specialty. To provide consulting services, add 2-5 more years.

According to Malcolm Gladwell, it takes 10,000 hours to become an expert at something. That is five years of work. With the shortage of knowledge in our space, I don't know how a great big software firm can put forth a one-size-fits-all C/ETRM suite and sell it for much more, save they are selling it to existing clients who have big wallets.

I have worked on three separate accounting software projects, two of which were large. I have seen that they all had many of the same hurdles to overcome. It is prudent to surmise that growing pains are organically absorbed, and maybe, in respect to the size of the client and the C/ETRM function in relation to the rest of their business, expectations may yet still create a positive perception for their clients.

Perception within our space, amongst C/ETRM firms, varies widely. Ask someone from periphery risk or logistics systems, and there are choice words I would not share here amongst our own brethren. Some founded, some really not. Perception, rather than truth, though, is what people see. The truth only comes years later, just as I experienced with my relatives after leaving Enron.

If a mega software firm wants to purchase and integrate a C/ETRM vendor, or class thereof, a traditional C/ETRM system is the best choice, rather than attempting to build-out the commodity and energy space in-house. A hard one to discern again, but if you are able to go to an existing client who paid you $1.6 billion for your accounting system, another $125 million for an energy suite is just an add-in. Or, a $435 million previously implemented ERP system and asking another

$35 million, may seem more easily achieved than buying a C/ETRM system for a proposed $18 million.

Standardized Software Platforms

Small- to medium-sized firms have found tremendous value in having the up-and-coming C/ETRM vendors provide a standardized platform that is much easier to implement and maintain.

Standardized being that each system has every client on the same version; no separate branch codes. These companies, depending on their niche and/or stage of growth, may also provide some customization, but it is usually to address the critical path of a transaction – not the Triple-A approach of giving you the *any, all,* and *automatic* software solutions the larger firms desire. Balancing the must-haves and the nice-to-haves with cost, is how many of these standardized software firms are able to deliver crisp solutions.

There are many firms who have purchased the major C/ETRM systems that should have definitely explored this avenue. There are also many firms today who are using bigger platforms, who may want to consider these solutions as an experiment for one segment of their business.

If you look at these up-and-coming software vendors' websites, you will see they have small players, but you will be surprised too, that they have large trading houses on their client list. There is no doubt some large players are leveraging and experimenting with standard software.

The Ultimate Future State

In the next five years, for the client who can no longer afford to lag, the choices are challenging. If you are waiting for the AAA – any, all and automatic – system capability, you will get replaced with someone who has started experimenting and who bought a system. The increase in big data needs and more complex sophisticated valuation tools that interact seamlessly with logistics are the keys going forward. Integrating these key factors into a core transaction processing system will follow.

There are definitely those who think this will be achieved sooner than 2020, and it is possible. Although we are changing at a faster pace, it still takes time to get where we all want to be.

We will get there though. By 2030, there will be no more than 3-5 major C/ETRM firms, plus the up-and-coming firms. Consolidation, fading into the sunset, and large software firms will dominate. Those that remain will be a legacy existence, with half-baked support, if any at all. A few up-and-coming firms will actually be one of the last standing, but if they don't also have the back-end accounting capability, they will be absorbed or vanish as well.

For more information of how **Front-2-Back** Consulting can serve you, and for some bonus information and downloads, visit:
www.frontmidback.com/book-bonus

Chapter 4: Industry Talent

Industry talent is an issue that has to be addressed when considering the spectrum of possibilities, not only when buying systems, but in our industry in general. This has always been an issue since I started in energy trading in 1994.

There is never an issue, though, that we are long traders. Nearly everyone wants to be a trader, one day. The allure of money, living on the edge and feeling successful ensures there is never a shortage of talent in the trader pool.

When I say industry talent, I am speaking of people who know more than just executing a trade, or who have done more than spend a lifetime trading corn or naphtha. I am speaking of people who have experienced multiple products and who have experience with more than just the basic transaction.

Yes, risk expertise to the quantitative side is an issue.

Broader than that, though, experience that has seen at least the back- and mid-office, in both financial and physical trading aspects, is lacking considerably. Add the software side of the business, and it is clearly where we continue to have shortages of talent.

Why?

Long hours in the middle- and back-office, the multiplier affect I mentioned earlier, and the accounting processes. I liken an ability to work in these conditions to a special forces operator who lasts 10 years, then burns out in many fashions and forms.

In the software arena, since I have worked directly in all roles, as you know, I think, for some, it is even harder. Traveling plus constantly changing cultures plus project pressures, equals a higher than average turnover.

I do not have a solution, but I do have a reputation with people half my age of trying to help them grow faster in this arena. I'll give you half a dozen younger, brilliants folks in the last few years who will give you their straight away opinion.

Unfortunately, I hate to burst their bubble. I have chosen a deliberate path to help clients first. And that requires very experienced commodity and energy trading and risk talent to make client success a reality. Clients are generally not that receptive to the younger, though smarter, crowd.

Overall, we are going to continue this problem of building talent for the future. Markets are changing at a faster pace, software vendors are scrambling to get ahead in a saturated market, and consulting firms repeatedly promise the same six staff on untold projects. Save they can clone those folks, disappointment is certain.

For more information of how **Front-2-Back** Consulting can serve you, and for some bonus information and downloads, visit:
www.frontmidback.com/book-bonus

Chapter 5: Big Data

"It's not if, but when," is a line I picked up –
from Warren Buffet – from an annual report
twenty years ago.

There are many who are frustrated that more
data, at more granular levels, with 21st
century valuation techniques are not
available today. It is an old story from Enron
days that has continued throughout my
career.

There are those, like me, who do not see this
as an issue. I see this as a major risk, not a
minor one. I won't say certain markets have
a greater need than others. That provides an
easy out for those few. The reality is that data
needs are going to grow exponentially in the
next decade.

Companies sitting on spreadsheets, great big
ones, are going to be caught with a major
catching up and a costly endeavor. That is
because some companies are holding onto
isolationist concepts that they hope will stay
the same until they retire. I understand that

thought. My reply, though, is what footprint are you going to leave? A carbon footprint or a footprint for everyone to follow, even decades after you retire to Phoenix?

I am not selling anything here either. I am an economic-based thinker and want to ensure we create optimal, risk-reward economic outcomes for trading and risk strategies and trading and risk software.

If your organization is behind on the basic systems, it is going to be harder to leap through the continuum of the 1990's to the present day. It gets harder each day you don't at least bring your data into a warehouse. And if the company has not experienced a software project in over five years, there will be fewer who have project experience. For example, in learning organizations, people who have experimented to full software process and system replacements will do much better in managing to get through projects; whereas, those who have little to no software project experience will not learn how to do projects in batch-mode, or play catch-up from 20th century systems, very well.

Some experience gained now goes a long way when you get deeper and deeper into understanding system needs, as you take those initial steps into buying and implementing software. That is why I do not care what state you are in today. I always ask, "What specific area is giving you the most headaches?"

The response, which I have said earlier, that I get from the triple-A trading personalities, is that they want any, all and automatically in the functionality or they don't want it.

Iterations are necessary in growing any business. Big Data is going to be a major step for many companies. To some, I say bring your mountain climbing gear. I have some experience in hiking and climbing Colorado 14'ers. That is not a picnic, even for many experienced high altitude sporting challenges. Therefore, let's get started climbing some small hills first.

In 1995, just out of grad school, I was one of the lucky few who had a Sun Microsystem computer on my desk. Yes, I was one of the big number crunching gurus tasked with analyzing correlations and volatilities for oil and gas markets.

With that luck, I also got assigned an ad-hoc request to create a monthly cash-flow of our trading books through its 27-year duration. However, the trading books were so large they wouldn't fit onto an excel spreadsheet. I received a beta copy of Excel 5.0, which was the introduction of 'subtotaling' thankfully enough, but the data-set was still too large to download directly into 5.0, so IT had to divide the data into 5 or 6 separate downloads.

Though it was a sign, one of many, thankfully, I only stayed at that job for two years. Fast forward through my energy trading career, from risk to trading to buying, installing, and consulting on untold software projects, and the issue remains the same. ETRM systems still cannot calculate timely, nor with useful models (i.e. black-scholes is old school) to the satisfaction of the cutting-edge trading leaders.

Specialized bolt-on software to crunch hundreds of thousands of simulations or to process an MTM calculation with 30 million rows to any satisfaction – especially in this elusive idea of 'real-time' profit and risk results – has yet to finds its way into core ETRM systems. This has frustrated innumerable clients.

With the volatility of markets today, and with markets changing faster than ever, and that we are on the cusp of revolutionary changes in the Power markets, and the even greater need to do cash flow projects, tomorrow we will wake up to the fact that we need billions of rows of data. We're calculating real-time correlations, volatilities, physical optimization, power storage possibilities, weather simulations, cash flow, risk, feedstock, and switching opportunity costs (to wind, solar, battery, oil, natural gas, hydro, or geothermal). A black-hole seems more easily understood than the challenges facing ETRM systems!

Are you ready to give up and succumb to a fate where we never catch up, not to the speed of light, but with the speed of change and Big Data times?

If you are still not convinced you need Big Data, look at the niche players who model sophisticated mathematical simulations using auto-regression, Geo-Brownian Motion modeling of spot and forward pricing, volatility and correlation, as well as weather data. Yes, simulating weather data. Take into account that companies are already segmenting consumer markets and behavioral sciences, human nature is already starting to be used to price consumer markets, especially in deregulated retail power and natural gas markets.

Today, though, we still have many utilities on spreadsheets just buying enough natural gas and/or power to cover their expected demand, and simply entering into spot markets to buy/sell the power and natural gas they need on any given day. That is simply the just-getting-by, old-school approach for with 20th-century thinking and application.

The question for you is: Where do you stand today? Are you satisfied with just getting by? What footprint are you trying to leave – a carbon one or a great legacy for others to follow?

Big Data is on our door step, ready to be unpacked. **Front-2-Back** believes there are ETRM software companies that are moving quickly into the Big Data arena. Others already see their own wake, and it may be too late. Said another way, ETRM systems have to get the next level, beyond basic transaction processing, without the old-school models, and take us into the 21st-century software needed to be successful in this ever-changing commodity and energy world.

Change is rapidly increasing, leading to greater volatility. Volatility equals risk. Risk equals reward – the free-market way. Get onto this wave and ride it into a winning market position!

For more information of how **Front-2-Back** Consulting can serve you, and for some bonus

information and downloads, visit:
www.frontmidback.com/book-bonus

Chapter 6: Valuation Models

Black Holes vs. Black-Scholes

I have specifically carved out a chapter for valuation, as it is never ceases to be an important part of any system and any trading and risk management strategy.

The dichotomy of this area is that we have many basic valuation tools, including some old-school tools that became the norm. Even with greatly known limitations, it was the best we had. Now, in the 21st century we are seeing more and more people moving to big data simulation – stochastic techniques that unleash the tail-risk, provide much better insights, and generally provide much better information than ever before. We also have many companies who are building home-grown systems.

Oftentimes, though, these systems take years to develop in-house, even if you buy them off-the-shelf, as someone has put years into the process. The challenge for many companies is the complete lack of these tools, but also where the pendulum has swung so far that 25 risk staff are taking models to a point of diminishing returns. We then end up knowing more and more about less and less. That may be humorous the first time you read it, and the second. After building and consulting for years, this is no laughing matter.

Senior management is often confused about many ideas these models put forth. The complexity, or rather that executives do not use these models every day, makes communicating the results more challenging. Communicating what those models do, much less getting into the weeds of every last input and error term, isn't effective.

Executives don't have time for the details, the tactical challenges you face, or the debates the risk folks are having amongst themselves. Focus on building what I call a "Picture of Risk," and communicate that picture. State the key outcomes with a broad brush, a few implications of 2-3 scenarios, and leave them with the information to digest later. Purposefully communicating the risk and opportunity is key, not solving a mathematical problem only university professors care to discuss.

Finding the best middle-ground solution therefore, means it is better to buy than build. And get off of the old-school valuation tools and into what is commonly known as Physical Optimization tools – tools that perform auto-regression simulation analysis modeling financial and fundamental data inputs, with big data crunching capability, that provide much better results to maximize your risk-reward profile.

Purchasing an out-of-the box system is exponentially much cheaper than trying to build one yourself. Sure, you can request a small change to their models to fit your internal modeling approach.

This is not to say these more sophisticated tools are impeccable. Impeccable is incongruent with human nature and the increasing change we face in all directions. For the cost of the system and implementation, these systems work very well. Getting the cash-flow-at-risk is an important attribute, not just the valuation. The gross-margin-at-risk is another. Better credit results too. I could go on.

What derails some of these projects, just like C/ETRM ones, is that often the data provided is suspect and the client doesn't know it. I have been on projects where the client believed their data was good, only to discover it wasn't. The data has never been vetted or validated, and when the results are put into these off-the-shelf systems, ETRM transaction processing to big data physical optimization systems, there are plenty of cases where the data is the culprit. Glaringly, I may add.

I do not disagree that at times there are promises that are not met by any tool. Hopefully, the ideas I suggest later in this book will help you assess not only the vendors, but the state of your systems and data. I am not suggesting even more consultants, but simply using the select few who have real experience in discerning results.

In summary, using 21st-century developed valuation tools is going to produce much better results, paying for themselves, in most cases, immediately. To get there, for many, and to overcome your tendency to model and debate every nook and cranny of the models, you will have to use the trading strategy from the last chapter of *Energy Trading and Risk Management* to really improve your state.

For more information of how **Front-2-Back** Consulting can serve you, and for some bonus information and downloads, visit: www.frontmidback.com/book-bonus

Chapter 7: Cloud and SaaS

Cloud-based solutions and software-as-a-service (SaaS) are certainly on the forefront of discussions. These solutions allow you to have your data and code off-premises, so to speak, via a web-based software service. You simply input and extract data and information rather than hosting the software on your own system. With a solution like this, you don't have to host the system, the data, nor do you manage hardware or software issues directly.

It is certainly an attractive idea, but the big question for these products is cyber security. Not long ago, I would have suggested against these options until security is enhanced. However, recent advances in cyber security for products like these has changed my mind.

Your company's proprietary, in-house software and hardware systems and processes are probably more at-risk to hacking than many cloud solutions. Two software vendors recently said the same thing, and I realized I need to open my mind to this idea as well. Although this is the only area you have seen me hesitant to explore, I now think all options should be on the discussion table.

Companies are using or putting a lot of applications in the cloud, and doing it nicely. Everything from infrastructure, to backup, to Big Data, to file storage and backup recovery.

One of the main benefits of this route is that you have reduced the upgrade risk for your software tremendously. How many projects have thousands of hours of extra code written only into their company's platform? A lot. When the software vendor sends a patch or new release, it often doesn't work with the customized solution, so they are stranded on an older version. Yes, they can send in a support ticket, but those take a backseat, so it often takes a long time to resolve. If you currently have a C/ETRM system, you know the pain of just inserting patches and releases, much less upgrades.

The software vendor managing your business in the cloud is now accountable for all of these issues. Does that make you sleep better? Or, since you do not have all of the customized needs, are people screaming more loudly than ever that they need more?

People always want more, so balance the costs and benefits of functionality in the cloud, as compared to hosting on-site with lots of customization and the security issue. True, you can get cloud customization, but 35,000 hours of customization is challenging and costly.

I don't think the security risk is as risky as others do because I don't think your trading is as proprietary as you think it is. That perception has been puzzling to me for years, save Enron's, which was clearly proprietary for reasons that are now obvious.

Are there companies I have been to, or worked for, that I can see have some discernable trading strategies that one can replicate? Yes, but not most. If you have read *Energy Trading and Risk Management,* you know that a sustainable trading strategy is not a singular focus that one can just easily replicate. In many markets, I can't even use that information across the state line, much less in their own market to trade against them.

In some instances, though, I really enjoy working trading strategies. Why? If I have to referee rather than integrate, with minor changes, it means you are not aligned internally on the trading and hedging strategies, and we need to go back to prior lessons on trading and risk management to create a disciplined process. That is why I wrote that book first, and recommend it before diving into a software project. Don't get me wrong, I enjoy trading strategies, developing them, and creating the book structures to support the reporting roll-up.

I will add that if your position report gets out today, someone may think, at first, they have something of value. They will quickly realize they probably have nothing. I know many would challenge that, but the trading debacles I have seen, not only in person, but also in the papers, are poor trading strategies and controls, not stealing position reports.

Also, consultants are too busy trying to make your project a success and not paying attention to your daily P&L. 99.9% of them don't care about your profits and losses, except that they do hope you are doing well so you can pay the consulting bills. As I have said, most don't know what a position report means, much less digest and run with it anyway.

Therefore, I think the cloud is going to flourish. And, in reality, the people hosting the cloud probably have much better knowledge, and capability in security than you do.

For more information of how **Front-2-Back** Consulting can serve you, and for some bonus information and downloads, visit:
www.frontmidback.com/book-bonus

Chapter 8: Selecting Consulting Firms

What's the Real Game Being Played?

This is one of the most under-estimated and under-achieving areas in delivering benefits to clients.

As a movie recently depicted, in interviewing a very famous musician, he says, "You act like I am a public official running for office. I tell the truth..."

I am not running for public office either. I am truly running an independent firm, giving clients and society the freedom of choice to discern the best solutions that benefit them and align with their goals and objectives. I am not putting my firm's goals first, as many often do. So often, I hear the frustration in the marketplace with great detail, from countless angles.

In being truly independent, and in being an expert – I have already shared my background of having worked both sides of the equation, and in every trading role – it amazes me that clients rarely review the consultants assigned to their project.

I have met with clients, especially when I worked a sub-contractor, only to discover that the client had no idea about my background and skills. They soon learned. I understand that the hardest part of any engagement is winning it, not delivering it. Don't discount that delivering is not hard – sometimes harder than it should be – it's just that often, winning the contract in the first place is even harder.

As a client, you have to trust someone and it often appears much easier to hang that hat on a large, long standing firm, rather than on a smaller, more personal trusted advisor and consultant. The perception is that it is safer to hire mega big billing machines to do the selection process. It sounds good and is easier in some companies to get internal buy-in. Mega consulting leaders have one goal, though. It drives how they provide this so-called independence – are they going to suggest a software product that takes 3-6 months or 18-24 months to deliver?

I see and hear the frustration of smaller, well-qualified software vendors who are getting blocked by big consulting. I, too, have seen it with major C/ETRM firms. Frustration everywhere. It is so easy in the demo phase to point out a few things one vendor's product doesn't have and keep the major issues with the one they are suggesting under wraps. When they are trying to sell a product, they only share the successful side of it.

There are some projects where I have seen mega big consulting do such a great job at selling that the project is weighed down by big billing machine consultants from the start. At the end, however, there are zero consultants at go-live. In other words, discern if commodity and trading experts are truly going to arrive as promised and see the project through.

I would like to share a story about this to provide insight from the consulting world. First, I just want to say, I am a big believer in free-market competition, but there is a line that I do not believe one should cross. I'll share the story and you make your own judgment.

Consulting Firm Intercept or Disruption?

Intercepting, disrupting, or latching on to a client is inappropriate and unprofessional in this business, yet I see it happening all too often. I have been on many projects with two or more consulting firms, and many times I have seen other consultants intercepting projects and disrupting progress.

I have seen situations where one consulting firm takes the client to dinner, and when the other firm finds out, they invite themselves by just showing up. But when it is the other way around, the self-inviting crew don't invite the other consultants. I personally have never invited myself to anything as I don't believe it is necessary or professional, at all.

In following that same pattern, I have also seen situations where a software vendor consultant will see that there is information or projects their two clients might want to discuss. Instead of connecting them to each other and allowing them to discuss their projects freely and openly, the third-party consultants act as a go-between, passing information between clients, but never connecting them directly.

The reality is, these are attempts to get consultants onto other projects, and intercept or disrupt a competing consultant's work. It does not allow for clients to connect, meet, and exchange ideas. It is purely self-serving as they don't allow their clients to gain a first-hand perspective from another client. Instead, they intercept the information, and present it in a way that makes them look good, and spins the information for their own needs.

I have even seen the situation get so bad that clients have had to tell consultants to stop having daily private meetings. And although they asked, the consultants continued these meetings. No one in that situation saw the end of the project.

Consultants and clients, together, are a team working toward a shared goal. There is no place for secrecy and private meetings on projects like ours. Intercepting clients and messages and holding separate and private meetings, are not in the best interest of the client. This is not professional nor fiduciary accountability to the client first. Or, any client.

Don't get me wrong, though, there are some very good consultants working at every firm. But there are also many who get sent along for the ride with great personalities and great deflecting skills, who seem to survive this consulting arena for years. They are fun to work with, but know very little of the industry.

When I was on the buy-side of software, and consultants were brought forth, either as the person doing the hiring or brought in to support me, I had the same perception as many of you reading this book. A perception that consultants were wasting my time and that I had to teach them my business. I didn't really know what they were doing with their heads in the bow-down into your computer mode all day, saying little. I saw many finally get discovered – that they knew almost nothing about trading, risk management, or accounting – after billing hundreds of thousands of dollars.

I thought, how could one ever want to be a consultant? Now that I am much wiser, it is exactly why I choose to be a consultant and why I will remain one for the rest of my career – I am a trading expert, front, mid, back and in software

I do not deliver the benefits of taking you to watch and/or play golf, unfortunately. Though, I certainly do take great pride in getting to know my clients personally, and staying in touch.

These are the reasons I stay focused on delivering benefits by keeping myself, and the entire team, focused on your needs. It is really quite easy to deliver when we never forget your needs, from day one to the end of the project.

To ensure our accountability to provide truly independent, expert advice, we publish our partnership approach with software vendors on our website. We will never block one software vendor for another, although we may clearly recommend one over another based on your specific needs.

Even when I have had disagreements with a software vendor or thought that a vendor's product that was not a good fit for my client, I have not blocked them. Why?

I don't control what they do, I control what I do. That is independence with expert capability.

Today, since every firm is growing and changing, history is history and I will bring any and all firms to the table that may be able to help you.

Everyone from consulting firms to software vendors has some value to offer, and I am just putting forth what everyone in consulting and in the software vendor world knows — there are plenty of players who are not going to provide objective, nor expert advice that benefits you. Instead, bringing you their big billing machine tactics and objectives that benefit only themselves.

For more information of how **Front-2-Back** Consulting can serve you, and for some bonus information and downloads, visit: www.frontmidback.com/book-bonus

Chapter 9: Transactional & Referential Data

One thing is certain: your data is not in the state you want it, nor is your reporting. That is the number one reason you want to integrate into one system. You are tired of the disparate set of data going, coming and not connecting. The integrity of your reporting has uncovered errors totaling into the millions.

The "busts" are there. You know they will come again. There is no panacea for data, it will always be an issue.

I continue to be amazed, though, at the state of data going into projects and how important it is to the success of any project.

The key to data is very simple. Tell me the reporting you need and the granularity, and you will know what data you need. Data, for clarity, that may need to be separated into 3 component parts in the new system. And, plenty of cases where data is just missing to meet the reporting needs.

If you can't deliver, in the requirements phase, a full set of reports with every data column provided and defined, you are going to be 'burning dollars'. A few will disagree with this concept. They will say it is contradictory, and that reporting is a design-phase project step. I hear ya. But all of us in consulting know reporting horror. Our mission isn't to maintain the status quo; it is to change the game.

The two things that need to happen before a project can be successful, are that you need to know which reports you require, and then the data you'll need to serve those reports, in that order.

Skip this step and you will find yourself spending millions more on your project than necessary. Spun another way, start with the end in mind, and the beginning will be much clearer.

Referential Data

This is the first data set that you must ensure is ready to go and load first. This data is simply the data that supports the transactions, trades, or assets you are going to load, or capture and process. Therefore, this data is essentially all of the drop-down choices one can insert on a trade, and many more data attributes that allows a transaction to process front-, middle- and back-office.

This is a key area in most projects that is not done well. Why?

It doesn't seem important to you, and most consultants want nothing to do with it. Everyone wants to escape this because this is the area that, if not done properly, timely and well, will send your project off the rails. Most never realize this is the underlying reason projects get delayed.

What everyone wants to work on is the supposed 'big stuff'. It is much safer to work on design documents, fiddle around, meet with clients, pass drafts back and forth, get coffee, and then hand the design specs to

97

someone else to insert or develop for the project.

That is how many escape connecting the dots on a project. I have seen industry veterans not know their own system. Put double digit years on their resume and clients think they know everything about the system. Again, it is great to suggest expertise, but doing the basics well still has to be a criterion, along with ability to solve more complex project problems. It is a challenge, I realize, to find someone with those capabilities, but it will cost millions if we are not discerning.

Someone has to know how to connect the dots and do the basics well. Bring me a consultant who can speak book structures, balance sheets and price indexes to physical optimization, and you have someone who knows the basics are more important to get done right, and get done right first.

Throw in those great big designs and their related extensions, and the dots are not connected. I have seen projects go completely backwards, where high-level consultants are staring, deflecting onto others as if they were the client themselves. Where is my bingo card?

Basic data is the issue. We will address how and why we will never make this mistake on your project, in the chapters on project planning and project execution. Wisdom will prevail.

Transactional Data

For clarity, the contracts with each counterparty is referential data at this stage of a project. When I say transactional, these are the trades which include the transportation trades as well.

The same concept applies here. Start with small sets of trade types, insert them, run them and check for errors before just loading all kinds of trades hoping it will work out. I have 99% confidence the first pass on any data migration is not going to end well. When that data migration is being done by someone new to the industry, it will end even worse.

Here is one simple question to determine if someone knows trading: ask them what is the difference between a trade type and a trade instrument.

For more information of how **Front-2-Back** Consulting can serve you, and for some bonus information and downloads, visit:
www.frontmidback.com/book-bonus

Chapter 10: Project Scoping: Everything is in Scope

Many projects start with the premise that they lack integration, especially in this business where one is still on spreadsheets or has disparate systems and data. Since the goal is integration, nearly every project starts with this mantra, "everything is in scope".

Everything is usually defined as everything we have today and everything we just dreamed up we will do for the next 100 years. Seriously, I have seen companies create lots of project proposals with "the next 100 years of capability will be delivered in this project". We may not do business in that product today, but we hope to, so include it in the project. Done!

I have seen everyone, from staff to senior leaders, make suggestions that in the 21st century, in 2016, all of this should be in the system already. So, show it to me in a demo.

Yes, bring your BS-bingo card to the demo. Magically, there are some software vendors who are able to suggest a functionality exists, and even fly through 30 screens showing you how to do it. Rather, how you could do it. Yes, they can.

It'll cost indefinite millions of dollars to deliver that, but it is true, they can show it. But can they make it work? Nobody I can find has ever lied giving a demo.

The reality, though, is that we generally assume it is already there in the product. Therefore, everything is in scope and the entire business we are in makes it even further into the system selection process. At this point, human nature creates expectations that are hard to overcome when reality meets the road ahead.

Process Reviews

It is worth noting that when purchasing software, processes will change materially with respect to specific roles, but will not change in the basic concept of front-, middle- and back-office transaction flow. To many,

102

though, since their role is changing, it may feel like the entire process is changing.

The reason is that there are still many companies who process data manually, along with process steps that are mitigating controls to ensure issues are reviewed, by traders, by mid-office, and by others, where in a new system these processes will no longer be necessary. With a new system, many mitigating controls cease and processes change, invariably.

For example, there are many companies where traders still do validations after a trade has settled to ensure the settlement is correct. Or where someone is taking data from multiple systems, especially in the back-office, and re-keying into settlement, reporting, and tax systems for their specific needs. Thus, roles will change, and you can expect to be more efficient and effective in the future.

After implementing a new system that integrates most of your data, this process review is more likely necessary in the selection process.

That is good to know, but more importantly, this is why I do not, unlike many other consulting firms, start scoping and requirements by creating numerous process diagrams and then linking those to requirements to ensure you have a complete set.

This is one of the greatest sales tactics big consulting firms use to bring more and more people to the table to help you connect the dots and create clarity for you. Or is it simply cash-flow for them?

Since the processes are going to change, diagraming a current state is not adding any value, it is typically just burning money. So, why do firms push this?

Two reasons: It sounds good, and the staff they send needs time to learn your business and trading and risk management, in general. It also furthers their ability to put people in place to begin building relationships. The latter is key to selling more, and it works.

If not convinced, show me half way through any C/ETRM project where those process diagrams, much less the requirements, are ever consulted, much less used to help design the new system and I will amend this book to include the one data point where they were used. Yes, I will get some emails and some pretty PowerPoints slide presentations. Those 30,000-foot pages could best be used to create airplanes to fly around the office. Those who find value are the new consultants you needed to hire to replace the ones you found had no idea what they were doing. They don't count.

It is why I start with the end first, then the data needed to meet the end, then I move on to the functionality required. The calculations, valuations, and iterations come next. Only after that does the process come.

That alone just saved someone at least $1 million!

For more information of how **Front-2-Back** Consulting can serve you, and for some bonus information and downloads, visit: www.frontmidback.com/book-bonus

Chapter 11: Defining Requirements: The Behavioral Science and All of Those "A" Words

We are going to start defining your requirements. Since we are now convinced through demos – even if you haven't even seen one yet – and with expectations that everything is in scope, we just have to ensure we communicate it in this phase so that we, as consultants, know what, where, when and how to deliver it to you.

Since everything is standard in trading too, a quick one-liner for each requirement will suffice. That's the mental model, for many. I have walked into, or rather inherited, project requirement phases to discuss, assemble and communicate the requirements.

AAA

This is not a credit rating or a minor-league baseball league. Now that we are still traveling in the anticipative state of expectations, a wish list is still embedded into everyone's mind. Let me help you get that onto paper.

The first three words out of a user's mouth is give me this with "Any", "All" and "Automatic". The triple-A request is the easiest to communicate.

Oftentimes clients communicate, in this phase, that until you do have the triple-AAA functionality, let's hold off – from the perspective of entertaining any system, down to specific components and modules – until the system does provide 100% of their expectations.

One of two things will happen for those who have these expectations: you won't be around, one way or the other, or you will finally realize you must move forward by phasing-in or accepting you can't have everything.

I do not specialize in triple-A projects. I do know of consultants who do, and I will gladly send anyone who thinks they require AAA to my competition. I hope those consultants accept those projects; it will keep them busy and away from clients who understand compromise and that they can get the benefits and value they need from a phased-in, focused approach.

Yes, this expectation occurs, even in markets new to trading like renewables, that the software vendor will just crank out the code for *any*, *all* and do it *automatically* so you don't have to.

If I said to you, "You can't have any, all or automatic," you would throw me out and hire another consultant. After about the 3rd, 4th, or as Dave Chappelle says "Fizzafth" consultant, you will discover that *any*, *all* or *automatic* didn't just apply to renewables but the rest of the project too, you will finally hear me and the other pros who have written the same thing. Wisdom will come, one way or another.

Since you are reading this book you clearly have humility or you wouldn't have paid for it. You know there are limitations and that you need others to support you to achieve any, all and automatically to reach your business objectives and goals over the goal line.

Therefore, as most consultants would do, I keep billing, I mean I keep my rinsed and re-used requirement templates together. You know, the ones that seem to show up at every project, by putting down *any* and *all* things, *automatically*, without fail. Cha-ching...

What is this accomplishing?

When I was, 31 and leading a large group of 25 or so, my boss said to me, "You can't fax your experiences to people." As if at 31, I had any to fax. At 51, I have a few, and I know more and more about less and less. But I have lots of grey hair which equals some wisdom.

As we continue moving through your project, you cannot communicate all of your experiences and wisdom, from the entire leadership team down to the front-line supervisors and staff.

What to do? Most keep on going.

What usually happens is that most every project goes through a phase of defining requirements to achieve the perceived company objectives. Directionally, they are.

They just do not know they are creating unrealistic expectations that, in turn, create a tremendous amount of frustration for staff and supervisors, including executives.

I was on a project, once, and when we were in this stage, the CEO had met with several internal key project owners. She said, "You know, 50% of projects fail." They heard her but were convinced they were different. Of course, by now they could write a few chapters here themselves. The point is, it is ok to make mistakes and sometimes play the fool, but when it turns to mockery, I walk into an executive's office and have a conversation. It's not our first either, since I don't sell projects to line supervisors.

Why? Executives have to clearly support a project. Approving and supporting are two different things. Executives and I need to have an understanding, and I have fiduciary responsibility, that I have your best interest at heart. And I do.

If the software vendor, who is trying to win your business, can't show in a demo that something is possible, someone else's demo guru will, and they will win your frustration – I mean your business – and get to collect those precious checks.

I had a leader once say to me, "I don't mind walking backward to collect that check." Well, for me, I do mind.

My point is that the feedback time between scoping and requirements and the project kick-off is so long, that by default of human nature, you start to have high expectations. Since nobody has said anything earlier – like that you can expect to get up to 85% of what you are asking for at best, with one system – each and every person is trying to figure out who misunderstood or who lied to whom.

I think it will be hard to rid human nature of stretching the truth. The key to knowing when something is unusual is when you ask a question, and instead of a demonstration, the response is simply, "We can do that." If that happens, be curious and follow-up. Although they aren't lying, I assure you many of them will require many millions to complete. Some problems will never be solved as they will need to change the software code.

To solve this expectation dilemma, we need a game-changing approach to product scoping and requirements to help you save many millions of dollars and opportunity cost. And disappointment at not receiving the project benefits you expected.

Does this mean we should document all of our processes with diagrams and connect the dots from them to the software before we buy it?

That would basically mean you were testing the system before you even bought the product. There will be plenty of attempts after you buy it for your staff and line managers "to

113

get it done before they start," which doesn't work well either.

But do you need the process diagrams to really validate that your processes will fit into the new system? No, you don't. I reiterate this point for clarity.

Here is a compromise: you go through the requirements and label each as a "must-have" (MH), "nice-to-have" (NTH), or "not required" (NR).

Using this method moves us to thinking about whether we really need certain functionality and determine if it is just a nice-to-have to make someone's life easier. An unrealistic example is a request that any, all and automatically the reports I use each day just show up in my email inbox at 7am.

Seriously, I have had that request. I asked, would it be better if I provided all of those reports to pop-up automatically at any time you log on to your computer? Yep!

This is how projects get sold into the millions. The bigger the expectation, the bigger the perceived value, and the bigger the software and consulting bills.

To be politically correct, that is what is perceived as selling value. Then, as the project starts to go off the rails, there are reasons to remove most of these features.

We have to take this even further, though, to get to realistic requirements. We need someone who actually knows the front-, mid- and back-office, who has worked in the industry, not just as consultant. One who can truly connect the dots.

I reiterate, too, that we have to ensure we know two things: the beginning and the end.

We call it customer-to-cash, but do any more than a few consultants really know what that means? It just sounds good, and most of us are still trying to figure out what it really means, much less deliver it.

The closest we can get to the requirements when we don't know the beginning and the end, is to at least know the end. Knowing the end allows us to create the beginning.

But wait, the project is being sponsored by the front-office, you know all of the people who make the money and believe, especially if they haven't worked in the middle-office, and they also need to know all of the reports needed, front-2-back and internally and externally.

When I say reports, I mean all of them. And, guess who has the majority of the reporting needs? You guessed it. The back-office has so many reporting needs that clearly the majority of the reporting comes from them. Financial reporting, to start. Regulatory reports going to government agencies, tax reports, payroll, SEC, exchange, FASB formats and rules, IFRS rules, internal rules, and for pro-forma needs. And then you've got balance sheets, income statements, cash-flow statements, three years of history compared, compared to budgets, compared to competitors, and, in the format the banks want to see it: the annual report formats. My favorite reports are for Dodd-Frank and Sarbanes-Oxley (SOX).

Ok, so we have all of the reports, the data attributes for each one, and we are 100% good to go. We are now so far ahead of most of any projects on the planet.

This does not address, necessarily, all of the process steps and buttons needed to push to make data move through a process and move into the final reports. To get all of the reporting needs, and the data needed to support the reports, we do have one more trick up our sleeve to further flush out the software capability.

It's not in this book. When I take you this far, it won't take long to isolate where the software issues are. Completing the analysis won't take more than a week, if that. I am hedging here. It should take me no more than 24 hours to tell you how many requirements are not met.

Requirements Examples

A few examples may further help you develop and understand your needs. Where these are not going to provide certainty, they will help you flush out what you need to know. Moving on to the vendor selection process is the goal here.

1. **Requirement:** Capture assets as options
   Description: Capture, value, report and settle, where appropriate.
   Requirement Level: Must-have
   1.1.   Capture all assets and long-term plant agreements as options
       1.1.1.Capture each unit per plant
           1.1.1.1. Insert all fixed and variable cost by unit
   1.2.   Value each with the Black-Scholes Strip Spread Option Model
       1.2.1.Provide Greeks in a drill down by asset, and unit
   1.3.   Value each with a simulation analysis
       1.3.1.Provide Greeks in a drill down by asset and unit
   1.4.   Value each using auto-regressive techniques
       1.4.1.Provide Greeks...

1.5.   Value each trade down to the 15-minute increment for the duration of the trade, asset-life, or contract.

1.6.   Report on all of the above using any method and provide it by the book structure with 7 levels, down to the fixed and variable cost per unit for any time frame.

2. **Requirement:** Provide all reporting attributes for each trade
Description: All trade attributes are captured on trader report
Requirement Level: Nice-to-have

3. **Requirement:** Physical and financial position report
Description: Ability to see trader position in one view
Requirement Level: Must-have

4. **Requirement:** Daily MTM report for MTD and YTD
Description: By trade, trade book structure, trader
Requirement Level: Must-have

5. **Requirement:** Ability to physically schedule trades by the hour
Description: Schedule trades for next hour, day-ahead and out 20 years

forward.
Requirement Level: Must-have

6. **Requirement:** Slice and dice position reports
   Description: Re-arrange report as needed for each user
   Requirement Level: Must-have

7. **Requirement:** Hedge accounting treatment for each trade
   Description: Capture and report on each trade
   Requirement Level: Must-have

I can sit here all night and type out 1,000 requirements, though the format you will see is usually a specific spreadsheet – one that seems to magically appear at every client. LOL.

I am using a format that does allow for drilling further into the requirements. The reason I used it is to show you on the first one why you will never get more granularity than I've included in numbers 2-7. The more info I put forth, the more likely the requirement will take forever to create.

Most importantly, the more info you put forth, the greater the chance the system won't do it. Number 1 cannot be done by most systems. Although I've used this format successfully, I had to keep complete control to ensure it did not turn into a page for every requirement. At that point we would be getting into designing. It is a balancing act will have to manage. And now you can probably internalize further how a list of requirements can turn into a wish lists, and that the requirements are most likely just a way to keep sales processes moving forward. Let it, as I have uses for these when it comes to finalizing software deals and consultants.

For more information of how **Front-2-Back** Consulting can serve you, and for some bonus information and downloads, visit: www.frontmidback.com/book-bonus

Chapter 12: Software Vendor Selection: The Art and Science of Momentum

If you've been in this industry for a while, you know you can't rely on what a software vendor delivered ten, five or even just two or three years ago.

Why?

Every client and every software vendor has had to customize their product to meet specific needs and the changing market, so it is nearly futile to go with who was ranked number one five years ago.

You have to discern which software vendors have been working in and around your space the last few years and narrow the playing field to only those – and I mean *only* those.

Do not allow someone who has been playing in the space for ten years, but has had no new clients on your playing field. Their equipment, so to speak, will be full of wooden bats, worn out gloves, a half working scoreboard report, and older functional requirements.

The other suggestion I will make, contradictory to what all others will tell you, is that when you find that a software vendor who has been playing in your space the last few years, you should call their clients and get 'references'.

Well, yes, and No!

Yes, certainly call and ask all the questions you can about everything from functionality to project selection to implementation. No company is going to give you everything, but you will get enough direction to discern how things are going in major functional areas. That is the key!

What was the scope, what functional areas were implemented, and which were not. This is much more important than knowing all of the small concerns in one area, and not getting the full spectrum of scoping with a broad brush. But when you find that a software vendor screwed up this, promised that, and that your competitor is completely unhappy with them, does that mean we punt that vendor?

No, we do not. Why?

You should be thanking the heavens when someone in your space has taken the plunge into a C/ETRM system in the last few years. They, no doubt, have had to "bleed the way" to bring a software platform into some very basic, and some complex, functionality on their dime, not yours.

Therefore, a bad reference means very little in itself. It may be they paid the depreciation, so to speak, and paid for your R&D. That would be the best case, and we would have to figure that out. They helped pave the way for the vendor to now be able to deliver an excellent product, without the hassle. Now you understand what I mean by momentum.

Another avenue that demonstrates momentum is how each vendor is preparing for the future state, as I said earlier. I would watch who is buying, selling, changing leadership, and I would look at what those players delivered historically.

Although I won't mention names here, I do watch what is going on in the market, and who has done all of the above and more.

I certainly see a couple of companies, over all others, that I think have the potential to become major leaders in this industry. It is not biased for any reason – it is just I see what they are capable of doing. However, I know these companies also have basic limitations in some product arenas that easily gets them removed from the short-list.

Due to their leadership, down to having visited with them, I may think it is prudent to work with them, and/or to wait for their product to improve through one of your local competitors, who are willing to pay the R&D costs.

Vetting a software vendor is rather difficult in this industry, but there are several more items that will result in a better solution over the other.

In this section of the book, I will therefore take you from the summary level, down to the major process areas, front-, middle- and back-office listing some key functional areas, including the things you need to really look at in selecting a software product. I will also provide some alternative avenues for making the software selection. The goal in doing this is not to provide concrete answers, but widen your thought process in how to select software.

Software Demonstrations – The Demo

There is no doubt you won't begin digesting the capability of a product without seeing it. However, "Belief and seeing are both often wrong," (Robert McNamara former CEO of Ford and former Secretary of Defense).

I have seen demos done very well and some done very poorly in the last year – and for the last 22 years. I have seen anyone from the CEO to a general staff member present the product.

No doubt, first impressions drive the sales process. I know products that have been around for decades that were recently not demonstrated well, and I have classified their potential to a lower status in the front-2-back transaction processing space, but not for other specialized needs.

However, the demonstration is one of the biggest wastes of time that can't be avoided. Staff show up and start asking one-off questions and these sessions go of onto tangents, making the process take too long, and making it unproductive.

There will always be the person who asks some tough questions that spur vendors into scrambling around on their lunch break inserting bogus information that will not work just to appease the question and move the sales process forward. I understand why they do this, because if they don't, someone else will show it that way, knowing full-well the functionality does not exist.

We can't void ourselves of demonstrations because we cannot move your organization forward without showing them something. People just have to see it to get some comfort. We will show it to them and keep your internal process moving too. It is a necessary cost to include everyone, though not everyone can be represented nor their questions fully answered, even after you have purchased the product.

Am I hedging you?

No, and the reason is that when you buy any system, it will change your process, not the other way around. The system will drive the process and it will change up to 90% of the roles in your company. Therefore, how you process data today is not how you will once you implement a new C/ETRM system.

Proof of Concept

Requesting a proof of concept is absolutely the best thing to do before buying or upgrading your system. But there is one caveat: this will only be an option for focused silo functional areas. If there is some specific functionality you need to buy or upgrade, you can take the time to prove it with a few transactions in a test environment. Definitely take the software for a very narrowly focused test drive.

To test an entire company's requirements would be impossible. I have seen this request, and I have seen it go absolutely nowhere fast. Only if you have all of the scenarios and referential data ready for input would that work. It's nearly impossible, save the 1%.

Even though the system comes with referential data, I am 100% certain that the data in the system will not work with your referential data, in any form or fashion. Not even the counterparty name, or the units of measure, or any number of other attributes – the software vendor uses *gal* for gallons and you use *usg*. Better yet, you use 4 decimals to convert units while the system uses 2, or the system has 6.82 and you use 6.83. You expect that the new system is ready to do it your way too, but it probably isn't.

Overall, I have used proof of concept, and it has worked well. I will use it again. I just want you to understand that the request that seems easy is generally not.

Proof of Concept Purchase

This is a little different than the general proof of concept. This is actually buying specific components of functionality you know you'll need, using it not only to discern the software, but to provide a learning platform for your organization to leverage into future projects. It is an approach I highly recommend. Many, though, want any, all and automatic, as I have discussed, but with that, the proof of concept would fail.

Proof of concept purchase is actually how I purchased the first off-the-shelf system in the late 1990's. A C/ETRM firm approached me with their natural gas logistics system while I was working in the oil space. I was young, but open minded and listened to their pitch. I said, what I really need is a financial derivative system because I have a book of oil and oil product puts, calls, collars, straddles, and a swaption or two, including both OTC and Exchange trades going out about five years forward. And we are about to trade Weather derivatives, too. Can you help me?

The response was, we don't have it but we can build it for you. But, we need you to define the requirements. And we don't have an option valuation tool. No worries, we already have the license, and I will put you in contact with them, I said, to bring it into your system as well.

I recall they delivered the system in 90 days. It was, however a front-office system where the trader input the trade, and we had some views but little reporting.

When it was delivered, it worked well and we just had to ask for a few reports, which guess what, we hadn't scoped and had to pay for – it was small and no big deal. No big deal as this was an experiment, a proof of concept.

The following summer, I had a college intern in the middle-office running the daily processes, interacting with the three traders, and the system worked very well.

Subsequently, we purchased it for physical needs, and helped co-create the oil logistics with this vendor, a vendor everyone now knows.

Add physical commodity or energy anything to any system though, and the world certainly gets much more complicated – nothing will be delivered in 90 days. You get the idea, though, that testing and experimenting is a viable route to pursue.

Free Trials

There are a few vendors offering free trials directly through their website. This is ok, if you are small trading house or have a very specific functional need, to checkout a software vendor.

It is certainly a way to discern how well the software vendor follows-up with you throughout. I'm not talking about regular canned emails. Is the software vendor calling you at least twice a week? Or are they calling every 2-3 weeks? Or not at all?

If you are a larger trading shop, you may be able to determine the same, but you won't be able to do this for an entire software package, front, middle and back, to run your entire business process on a free trial. Taking a few trades through the system may be useful, though, so ensure someone is free to focus on this endeavor.

I am not completely sold yet on the idea of free trials. There is just so much to a business process that no one person, save someone, like me, who has worked in every role front-2-back, can make a deep assessment. Maybe a high-level assessment, but definitely not anything more from a 30-day free trial.

The Software Sells Itself

I have heard people tell me, as long they get a demo with a client their software will sell itself. But since I know the software doesn't command millions of dollars, that is a fallacy.

When I shared the idea of free trials and the idea that the software sells itself, to other successful consultants, their responses were both, "Run!"

I am more open-minded than to run from anything, and we will see what develops with these approaches, but the point is you can't sell value if you are trying to give it away or just think your product is so good it'll sell itself. If it were that good, you wouldn't be talking to me, or anyone, about how you need this and that from my firm.

Software Vendor Roadmaps

I live in Colorado, so not only do I have a GPS and a PLB, but I carry roadmaps everywhere I go. I am navigating in unchartered, 12,600-foot territory in my off-road vehicle, or hiking, and I need to know what to expect.

What changes faster, markets or weather at 12,600 feet? If I need help, I have the PLB and will engage it, but it is costly. It means many more people are brought forth to help get me out of a predicament.

The roadmaps I carry are built to ensure I know my way forward. Working with software vendors is no different than hiking, you need to know the path forward.

If it looks like a brochure, it is. If your specific functionality is not on the roadmap, is it a stop sign, yield, or dead end, or does that trail even still exist? If the software vendor doesn't know where, when and how they are going, neither will you.

Patches, Releases & Upgrades

This is another area where you need to discern the viability of a software vendor. You want to know they are responsive to software issues. My iPhone gets updates constantly, I don't know what they do. I just hit accept and move forward. In the C/ETRM space, this is not a good idea unless you know exactly how the update will perform in your environment, not in someone else's.

The number of these releases is key too. Are they coming often? Does that mean they are responsive or reactive? Generally, it is not a good sign if there are more than 4 updates a year. More than 4, and even up to 12 is not uncommon.

The next question is how many branches of code are you using? That question is not likely going to get a quick response, but how they respond to that question will signal the answer. I have asked some vendors this question and have been immediately told everyone is on one branch, end of story. That is a good sign.

Again, I wish I could provide a magical answer to fit everyone's needs, but there isn't one. However, you can see I do not limit possibilities based on a perception. I will take you a step further and do the heavy lifting to help point you in the right direction.

I will walk you through a deliberate path to determine the software vendor's capability. Although this is still high-level, I may dive deeper on a few points, for illustration. I will touch on the major functional areas that you should discern quickly, and ones that many don't ask about, but should.

I'll present it with a little deliberate humor. It helps bring levity and will show you how to think differently. If you haven't been through an ETRM system purchase and implementation on both sides of the fence, as

I have, I will give you some comfort, humility and understanding like no other. We are going to move you into the 21st century, together, but I want to ensure we start with expectations on the same planet, if not in the same playing field.

For more information of how **Front-2-Back** Consulting can serve you, and for some bonus information and downloads, visit: www.frontmidback.com/book-bonus

Chapter 13: Front-2-Back Software Assessment Ideas

I have purposely used the word *ideas* in the chapter title, because I cannot know your requirements from a far. If I do have the opportunity to assess your requirements and software, we will have hundreds, or close to 1,000 requirements. Any more than that and you are either designing or overlapping requirements.

Once you have these requirements set out, you are ready for a software vendor selection process. Can you just hand over your requirements and expect the demo to provide the results? You can hand them over, but since they are the same template that seems to be all over the world, you need to take key requirements and ask some questions.

The key to asking those questions is not to check off each requirement, it is to gain perspective on both the simple and challenging requirements you have. Showing up with requirements in your head and a dozen other people, will send your demo off on tangents. Everyone wants to be heard, everyone wants answers today, and there are some who are going to derail the project before it even gets started.

Therefore, I will walk you through a scenario of questions to ask front-, middle- and back-office and provide some perspective. I use colorful word choices to help flush out the essence of the situation, not in hopes that it helps you get the answer, but to help you develop the wisdom to craft your own questions.

Front-Office Capability

I understand that what you want to see first is your position report, or what your view will look like. And, that you want to slice and dice the data anyway you want.

Done! Sold to the guy with the big fat wallet!

You can expect any system will have some canned views, and some slicing and dicing, to an extent. Even adding and re-arranging and saving the view for your desktop are done out-of-the-box. Done, sold, right? Not so fast.

Asking these questions will open the hood and provide you much better insight:

Has your software company's CEO read Mr. Berley's book, *Energy Trading and Risk Management*, especially the end?

1. Until they do, we will reschedule.

2. This is a note to most traders, the attitude from some vendors is extraordinarily the most curious thing you will ever see. Trust me. The egos in the C/ETRM space are huge, but until they act like the CEO I articulated in that first book, reschedule their demo. If you have yet to read my introduction, please go back and read so that you at least have some background on my perspective and approach to dealing with people.

Will you show me how many front-office reports you have? Great, please open them.

1. Can I see both my financial and physical positions in one view? Yes Ma'am, and Yes Sir!

2. Can I slice it any way I choose? You betcha.

3. Yes, will be the answer for any other similar inquiries. Don't stop now though, keep asking questions.

How many, and which, reports do your other clients use out-of-the-box?

1. For the majority, ranging upward and well in the 90th percentile, these reports, no matter how you slice, dice and re-arrange, will have to be modified. I know many consultants who all say the same thing: clients rarely ever use out-of-the-box reports.

   Why? Because the reporting will need to be customized for your needs, and be prepared to pay for them. There are no two trading shops who view the world the same. It is not the software vendors issue, sort of.

   Use a BI tool – generally not a great idea for front-office on-the-fly reporting needs. Especially with a position report. Even the out-of-the box reports may provide instant position reporting, save options are involved. BI tools are great for historical and accounting reports for internal needs, not usually trading reports; though one could customize some BI tools for front-office capability if so desired

2. Out-of-the box reports are generic and relatively few. Be prepared to sit down and craft your reporting needs, just like everyone else in the process is going to do before the software selection is complete.

Can I get real-time position reports? Yes, you can.

1. With real-time valuations. If no options exist and you are ok with yesterday's closing price, then yes you can. Why this is such a big issue, I don't know. You should know your position, and the approximate value change when the market moves. Having a report in real time should not be a priority.

2. I rarely gamble, but there is an old adage that you shouldn't count your money anyway. If you have a disciplined, healthy trading/hedging program, intra-day moves in many markets do not matter.

3. In Power, you may need real-time reports, but anywhere else, it's not even close to necessary.

What valuation tools are embedded into the system?

1. Those that don't know, tell; those that do, don't. For the most part, the valuation tools you need are only half-baked.

2. Bolt-on time. Get ready to buy a bolt-on system, here and three other places, especially in Power. If you trade options, it is really time to up your game.

3. Shadow settlement for Power. You can have this if you're prepared for yet another bolt-on system.

4. Trader marked P&L statements. You're fired. Score-carding is important, but we are about to spend many millions. If you have a finite budget, a personal scorecard is probably not a must-have. Use the book structures and trader slicing to mirror a scorecard to the extent that it's reasonable.

5. Credit reporting. You probably want a report that will warn you when you get close to your limit. But if you were close to your limit at the beginning of the day, that should be on alert already. You don't need your system to do that for you.

6. Trade entry. You might want the system to default the fields you use often. It's possible, but only if you want to spend your whole budget on it. If you do get it, which you can with some systems, when you are sick or on vacation, nobody will be able to enter trades on your behalf without your logon. Would that work for you?

7. How about any, all and automatic? Sure, just hand me the check book and pre-sign some checks.

Trade capture

it appears all-encompassing, show me!

1. Do not assume all of your financial and physical instruments can be inserted and valued.

2. Send the vendor all of your trade types in advance of the demo. Give

them some real data. They don't trade nor do they have time to see your data and tell the next client about it. They really don't care unless the trade cannot be captured, which is never an issue in a demo. Get that? Never an issue. The trade can be inserted in a multitude of ways, but that doesn't mean it will value, much less process or settle, especially for physical products.

3. Will the system allow you to insert all of the fixed and variable costs of your physical plants by unit? If you do have that granular of a need, be prepared to challenge that the system can do it, especially if it is going to be valued as an option. How those costs are captured and then valued, especially in options, will be something you need to see to believe.

4. Foreign currency. Again, every last trade type you engage today needs to be reviewed. Show me its price, in every form and fashion, and settle correctly. Timing differences here can really be an issue, especially if you price in one currency and settle in another. Spot, to forward, daily,

weekly, average, or whatever your need, send your trades for the demo.

Book structure and price indexes

1. I have lumped these two together as we search for disaggregation within a portfolio. You will find a varying degree of capability in this area. Ask to see how price indexes, in all of the products you trade, can be disaggregated, not just captured.

2. Book structure. At a high level, you can expect you will need to modify this, as most systems disaggregate in four to six buckets. Anything less and you may be able to use the out-of-the-box functionality. I have seen clients ask for six to ten layers with attributes underneath so they can slice and dice about 50 different ways. This not going to happen without major modification to any software.

   I understand that more and more companies want to disaggregate down to unit level, capture each fixed and variable component, and do it in a book structure. A fee structure is challenging enough for most systems, but to also have your internal cost structure embedded into the reports, you'll cross the line of capability for any system without modification.

3. Price indexes. Expect to disaggregate into a variety of components to get to the underlying most liquid products in your market. i.e. location, basis, price, quality. If not, the system is limited or you are in a less liquid market to take your price from Timbuktu back to Henry Hub, PJM, or Cushing.

4. Fee structures: I will also include in this section, for clarity, fee structures for contracts, tiered in fees, quantity, price, location, and grade, can be anywhere from simple to rather challenging. Find your most complex fee-based contract and send it in for the demo.

System performance

1. There is a simple formula to follow here. First, you are not getting intra-day, on-the-fly, reporting with current market prices and instant profit and loss statements. But updated positions, certainly. If you add options, though, you will have no update unless someone runs a valuation and loads

some prices with today's date on the feed.

2. Second, if your book is full of options, and especially assets modeled as options, it can take 15 minutes to process. In power, it can take several hours to run these calculations. Speed is always an issue, and I have mentioned this in Big Data. We will have an ever-growing need for Big Data, and the speed to go with it. Be prepared to take it upon yourself to discern how to parcel out tranches of trades into the database, instead of relying on your software vendor. Just a thought.

I have to pick on the front-office. If you have only been a trader your entire career, congratulations. You have felt little pain, save when you lose money. The rest of the process, and the company, are the real beneficiaries of most of these tools. They will do the heavy lifting, as you will soon learn. If you ever want to lead a trading shop as an executive, I suggest you take the time and make the effort to learn a little about how the rest of the process uses your data, and why when you don't provide enough detail in the design of the system, it costs you in the long run.

That is the secret – the hidden gem in buying an C/ETRM system. If they are included in this process, which is often an afterthought, the middle- and back-office will gain more than data integrity, they will gain much more data for daily reporting and analysis.

As we move forward, I am intentionally spelling out where issues occur in software selection. I want to help, not just to create realistic expectations, but to get people thinking in terms of asking and discerning the software capability by thinking through these examples and crafting ones that fit your business needs.

Middle-Office Capability

Risk
There is little chance your needs are met here from most C/ETRM vendors. Bolt-on. Next.

Middle-office daily control reporting

These are the folks who ensure all trades are captured, fix trade entry errors, kick-off valuations, show up first in the morning, and ensure the positions and P&L are ready and accurate for traders, leaders, accounting and compliance.

1. Can I embed your trading policy and associated limits into the system? Sure, in many systems.
2. Will it automatically notify someone when a limit is breached? Yes, but it will cost you.

Scheduling

1. Depending on the product, there are a myriad of bolt-on logistics software vendors, and ones even schedulers in their own market have never heard of.
2. I will say that the ETRM systems are making improvements to move products, but depending on how long ago – hopefully five to ten clients ago – they started developing each respective product area, you might get some basic functionality.
3. I would highly suggest providing the specific steps to the software vendor,

in advance, and have them demo your data.

4. In markets newer to ETRM, such as LNG or oil, there is pain on the street. As I said earlier, some are taking it for you in advance, so find those recent projects and the software they are using, and you may find a software vendor to put on your short-list.

Credit

Forget it. Actually, many are bringing their calculations into their C/ETRM systems with PFE, CE, PCE, and other data attributes to capture collateral and other credit rating attributes. Again, these will be mostly deterministic.

1. One caveat: The credit arena, as with scheduling, has a niche perspective and it is amazing how many credit modules are being used from a different C/ETRM vendor than the rest of the company. I have seen projects where credit gets scoped away after the project starts because the credit department just won't accept the software – it happens often. My point is, be aware and manage it to ensure

we are using tools with the
cost/benefit thought process.
2. Or buy a physical optimization tool.

Back-Office Capability

In this area, which is the big one, we have
to discuss a myriad of things to ensure there
will be no misunderstandings and that you
leverage these tools – and are on the project
team from day 1!

I have seen projects where the accounting
department is nowhere to be found. This is
the hidden gem, and the biggest little secret
of purchasing a C/ETRM system: the
reporting needs of the back-office are the
largest by far.

That means Finance has to fully participate,
from scoping to selection and through
implementation. Accounting has the biggest
data needs, not the front-office. If you are in
accounting you are saying, "Thank you,
someone has finally heard me!" If you recall,
I finished graduate school with a BBA in
finance and an MBA. But quietly, every last
elective I ever enrolled in was in accounting.

It is the reason, too, that the smartest guys in the room were still there 5 years after I left, and those smart alecks owed me $2.5 million. I know what off-balance sheet financing looks like – how to not only hide it, but take that 25% effective rate of interest oil prepay deal and create $25 million of P&L on top of that crazy loan. Add some more fictitious market-to-market, and you understand why I know when not to hold'em or fold'em, but to run. LOL.

We have to keep this in perspective, though. Just as the front-office has been duped by many a C/ETRM salesperson, so has the back-office. First, C/ETRM systems are not accounting systems, per se. Some do it better than others. With the right system, the shell to have a lot of accounting information is there to help you move data into information and to interface that information with other internal systems.

I would be remiss, though, not to dive deeper.

Chart of accounts

I have seen some scary-looking setups after certain players left the building.

You cannot use a C/ETRM system and expect that it is going to act like a general ledger or subledger, yet some inventory valuation capability is available. You can easily get your summary-level chart of accounts, but you are not supplanting or replacing the accounting/ERP system you currently have.

Settlement

I am sure for most this seems simple unless you've worked in this area. The number of attributes needed that don't make it this far in the process, if ever collected, cause a lot of re-work.

Formatting is probably the second most important issue. Those crystal reports, or whatever tool you use, have to be customized for you, not for the software vendors, so more consulting work is required.

There are some markets where settlement processes are not just daily, but intra-daily. Release a cargo, rail-car, or truck and an invoice is triggered. Many ETRM systems will require someone to manually kick-off a valuation, as the valuations usually are automated for daily runs. You can certainly program many settlement runs, but some folks prefer the manual intra-day method.

As we move the data through settlement, there is data that needs to keep flowing, but not necessarily on the invoice. Ensuring that it does flow behind the scenes, there will be more data attributes, some out-of-the-box and some custom columns. Be prepared to add many columns to ensure data is captured at the beginning.

It should be clearly noted that many firms do not have a standard revenue/expense recognition process. I have seen companies go in and out of unrealized, recognized and realized, intra-month. No two companies are alike.

Tax

This is an area that often requires a bolt-on. Rudimentary capability is generally in place, but taxes on taxes, or the ability to choose from a menu of options – exempt and non-exempt, product to product, jurisdictions, states, countries – can be much more time consuming than you know.

FASB/IFRS reporting

You may think something as innocuous as short- vs. long-term asset and liability reporting is out-of-the-box, but don't be surprised when it's not. There aren't a bunch of CPAs sitting around software vendors.

It may be interesting to know, too, that my definition, and your definition of short vs. long-term can differ as well. I have seen short-term defined as up to 18 months. To me it was a rolling 12 months in my trading books. Therefore, look for changes in accounting pronouncements while selecting systems. They will usually be behind in baking many of these into the system.

They will claim to have FASB 133, 157, 161 or IFRS 9, 32 available in some systems. Get a demo to prove it. Don't expect that a balance sheet, income statement, or cash-flow statement, in the accounting guru format, is going to exist in these tools.

Regulatory reporting
When I started in this business, regulatory reporting was certainly not going to make the cut for any system. That is why there are some bolt-on systems here, especially for hedge testing.

Be prepared to not have clear designations of hedge levels 1, 2 or 3. It will most likely be required as an extension or re-work to fit your needs. Some define these by trade types or price indexes – whatever the rationale, be prepared to see this issue early.

Hedge effectiveness testing. Yes, the user guide says it is there, but it doesn't quite work as you may think. Differing approaches, perceptions and applications rein it in.

Throw some of this data at the software demo. You now know why I hope you haven't gone through that phase. You will want to do it again, I assure you. That cost, not only to you, but the software vendor as well, is worth knowing up front.

Dodd-Frank reporting is even available in several systems. It will be basic, but it does suffice. For some, it is a nice-to-have where spreadsheets, for those who report quarterly and do not have tens of thousands of trades, would suffice. For others, it brings value in connecting to the repository of Neverland. You will probably get the main FERC reporting 556, but not likely FERC 745/55.

Therefore, if you think these systems are doing a great job of keeping up with all of the U.S. to IFRS standards, to FERC, NERC, and state regulations, don't have high expectations here.

Inventory
Valuing inventory is challenging for most, but you can rely on the information for booking. No doubt there are numerous

trader valuation methods that are constantly being updated, changed, or provided during a project. The iterations in the logistics chain may seem straightforward – it is either on the truck/rail/boat and in-transit, or it is sitting waiting to be offloaded, or it is offloaded. I have seen some interim steps here, though, that can add complexity and challenge.

The overall point for any of the above major process and functional areas seems more of a note of caution to ensure what works and that you definitely know your data attributes early to ensure they are baked, not re-worked after UAT, further delaying the process.

There are two key reasons finance can be the greatest beneficiary for C/ETRM systems: if you have accounting on the project early, the reports are clearly pre-scoped and pre-defined, and you will have already determined your data attributes. You will have all of the data and information you need to further the accounting process than you ever had before.

You may need a BI tool, a bolt-on for basic settlement views and some hedge accounting, and interfaces to your main accounting/ERP system, but you will have much more granular data to use and leverage, to add value in the back-office.

Contracts

It is amazing to me how companies have used this area, from basics to complex trades. If it's not clear, I have seen trades modeled in contracts due to unique trade language, like cross-commodity switching costs, almost as if they were options. To the client, they were simply contract attributes that needed capturing in some form or fashion.

Certainly, you will find many data attributes available in this area, but I see many businesses who cannot find all of their contract attributes in the system. For example, if you have 350 trucks and you lease those out to move the product, those trucks may represent 350 contracts you need captured in your system.

In what demo does the contract department get represented? Often the accounting department is not involved, so contracts are also usually left out.

IT department
I certainly have to visit this area with some wisdom. You already know every last interface, right? Most do. What most don't have is what I have said above: the data known. High-level scoping and requirements rarely provide IT with a starting point. IT ends up waiting months and months before the interfaces begin. Those generally take longer than expected.

I have written these technical specifications and they are a back and forth, multiple iteration, multi-month challenge – just to get the specs written, much less programmed. Add logistics and IT will be running around endlessly. Add the other areas from tax to trade entry, with assets modeled at a granular level for costing, and you are definitely going to be underpreparing IT for what is about to be thrown over their wall.

161

Add the data migration alone and that is overwhelming for many projects. The additional columns that usually come out of nowhere, 90% of the way through a project, and the re-work is just beyond expectation.

Regardless of which group I have mentioned, it always boils down to two things:

1. Reporting needs are not well defined, if at all.
2. Data needs, therefore, are not well defined, either.

They will need to not only manage this part of the project, but also the numerous releases, patches, back-ups, security and the extensions that make your system unique. Yes, these systems often have web services, but all of those extensions are going to be local to your system and cause performance issues as well.

User guides

I realize that most vendors are not going to release the user guides until you buy the software. When you do get your hands on

these, consider them like you are buying
food or medication. Huh?

Like food or medication, I would suggest
these user guides have mostly expired.
Check the date to see if the user guide has
been updated in the last year. *Of course, by
now, the vendors have read this book and
have updated all of their guide's release
dates.*

If these guides are more than a year old,
they are probably stale. If they are over two
years, you can be certain they are losing
value by the day. User guides are rarely
kept up. Code changes, especially with all of
the releases, mean the user guides are the
last thing anyone is thinking about updating.

I have seen user guides that depicted that
something worked, and I can tell you, it
probably never worked. Yes, the user guide
was better than the software!

Offshoring extensions
In the last few years I have seen more and
more of this used by clients and software

vendors, but also consulting firms, to win more and more of the work.

Offshoring itself is an issue. It's worse when the consulting firms, who are assisting you through selection, start mentioning they can also help with extensions because they offshore it to save money. Here is a great example of where those consultants lack independence.

Since I have first-hand experience, offshoring is not working well at all. For less than half the rate, the true cost is at least double the average rate. Why? These offshore vendors waste so much of the consultant's time calling the firm with uncountable questions, all day long. When I say all day long, I mean all day long. And, when you open the environment, it is in such disarray you can't answer their question.

Let me state for clarity, I have tried to help, and help beyond necessary because I like to solve problems. Americans give it 60 seconds, the Japanese 60 minutes, and I have taken hours. I have since stopped doing that, and now do adhere to the 60-minute rule of thumb. However, I am talking very basic things that are not done correctly offshore, and then you are off to the races chasing their problems in completely different time zones.

The real issue is that most all of these people do not know trading at all. They may know code, but they don't know trading, and it shows through so much I can't state it more than I have.

At this point, I understand why clients request professional liability, or what is known as E&O insurance, but this book alone should subject me to a free pass from ever buying this insurance!

Summary
I have only scratched the surface of functionality that one should explore in selecting a C/ETRM system, or any other class of systems mentioned earlier. I surmise, though, that I have given plenty of perspective to help you think about your

business in a way that truly uncovers the key functional areas you'll need to discern.

For more information of how **Front-2-Back** Consulting can serve you, and for some bonus information and downloads, visit:
www.frontmidback.com/book-bonus

Chapter 14: Project Planning: More Art than Science

There are many consultants and vendors alike who tout their project delivery as "agile" or always "timely". Many mention, too, that they have nearly 100% success and 100% track records in delivering projects. One of my favorite claims is that 100% of our clients are referenceable. My daughter and my pastor will give you 100% references for my firm too – so what?

If this were all true, why would they have to pay well over $200/hour for someone who has any real experience – above $300/hour is very common. Software company leaders charge well into the $400/hour for – due to being on 12-15 projects themselves – doing nothing more than sitting on weekly calls and stopping by once a quarter for a few days, adding little to no value.

Have I been on projects that have gone really well? Yes! Have I been on projects that have rolled off the rails before even getting started? Yes, I have! Everyone, apart from the client, knows it and just rolls with it. I know why this happens, and it won't happen with my firm. Independence, in its true state, provides trust.

I have seen projects achieve nothing for a year, and yet the client lets the consultants bill away until someone decides it is time to work. As I have said, and will say again, there are many consultants staring at their computers, few knowing what to do, when, where and how. There are others limping along, deflecting and attending as many meetings as possible to buy time.

To claim 100% success, as blanket statement – or even anywhere close – is a fallacy in a market that cannot meet more than 70-80% of your requirements. There are countless bolt-on classes of software, too, we have articulated, that can increase this percentage to the 85th to 90th percentile of expectations. Many clients are provided a nudge – a hint – that they may need these additional bolt-on systems.

Before the project kicks off – from a combination of not really knowing the system you are buying, internal perception and sales approaches – the suggestion that we can make one system work or that the vendor will complete their roadmap timely, or that we can solve this issue and 38 more with an extension, is generally setting oneself up for disappointment.

After project kickoff, many companies in the last year realize they must have, not a nice-to-have, these additional systems. A word of wisdom to consider this risk in your project planning. Based on these facts, when someone says they are 100% successful, it is either the companies who are only trading financial futures or one physical instrument at one or two locations. I am thinking of a project that is claimed to be 100% successful because it was below budget and was delivered basically within 90 days of the original due date. Sure, if you remove over 60% of the reports, you can hedge to that outcome.

Then, there are those who tout "agile", when it's really just chaos. If you are working on so many things at once, such as chasing referential data while you are in the design phase, it is certainly more chaotic than productive. In reality, that kind of chaos drives lots of rework. Re-work costs you time and money.

At the same time, scope creep occurs. It goes back to those original scoping and requirements that were gathered using the same coffee stained templates that have circulated from project to project. Since consulting firms and software vendors are just moving the process to a "software license close," these initial steps, which are critical to setting expectations, are often setting many projects up for failure before they start.

Often, they push you through the phases to, "just get it done," and move you toward a sale. But in my model, all of that comes later.

Before we really jump into project execution and focus on the critical areas of success, I would like to start here. Projects are prepared poorly for countless reasons – project leaders are assigned from other non-trading groups, with little time to work on the project and project tools are rarely used beyond the 25th percentile.

Oftentimes, the people putting the project timeline together are 'thumbing it'. You can't predict with certainty, and when all of the external parties involved, consulting firms and software vendors feel bad that you wasted your entire holiday break creating a 1248-line project plan that has absolutely no chance of success.

I have worked on projects where the requirements went into the thousands. And how far are those requirements going to see the light of day once the project begins? Rarely, save the few who actually phase their projects and do a requirements refresh in each phase.

One can discern a client's maturity the minute they want to do an overhaul of their entire financial and physical trading business. Not unless you are a small shop with few trades can this be done well.

With 1,000 high-level project tasks, and many not assigned, one should not be astonished when deadlines are missed. Getting a project task to 90% complete is only half the work. The last 10% is the hardest part.

Creating a perception of "done" is one I see used all too often, to make it appear as though projects are creating momentum when in fact they are not. The perception of momentum might be good enough for many, but it is not helping the project in any way. The perception of "completed" or "nearly completed" might meet the project roadmap, in the interim, but eventually the real outcome surfaces. Clients are disappointed and consultants are the only ones who win.

There is a simple thought process, before I suggest the critical path to simply follow, and that is to break the planning into short- and long-term objectives. The key is that the short term – for the next 2-4 weeks, at most

– should have specific people working specific tasks that align to the critical path I suggest. Sounds intuitive, but most projects don't get to this level of delegation, as people are flying all around the 35,000-foot level hoping something will get done by someone. Only 20% of the project staff do 80% of the work.

There are those who will say that the 20% who really deliver the work don't matter. When I first heard that, I thought that was absurd. Now, though, I can see if you follow what I am suggesting below that the 20% really doesn't matter if you manage the project properly.

There are examples of people who, having delivered countless projects in their career, on-time and on-budget, get frustrated that they were not promoted to CTO of a large company. Projects are hard, and sometimes even the ones who deliver well get a hardnosed reputation. That is what you asked them to do, they delivered it. The project team felt like they were run over to meet the deadlines. I assure you most of the people who are working on subsequent projects appreciate it and wonder where that go-getter went – because the project they are on now is dragging along with no end in sight. Bring the wisdom back please.

So, how do you balance deadlines with people and the human nature that always surfaces? I have this concept of keeping it simple, and keeping the project lean, especially early on.

Assign tasks and deadlines with short durations and find out who can deliver what, when and how. Find out quickly who is really doing the leg work and who is deflecting so you can weed out the politicians. There are people great at deflecting to the software vendor, or the client. Let me be clear, in the consulting world it is not just politics, but a sporting event, every single day. At 32, I would have been frustrated. At 51, I laugh.

For more information of how **Front-2-Back** Consulting can serve you, and for some bonus information and downloads, visit: www.frontmidback.com/book-bonus

Chapter 15: Project Execution: *Basics* is the Name of this Game

There are certain tasks you MUST do here to launch a project into a state of *momentum*. When projects find momentum, the people working on that project find great satisfaction and some even have fun. You just know when that's happening – it feels good. Many, though, have never been in this zone, so let's get it together.

This priceless book, will save you millions of dollars, create buy-in sooner than later, and escalate your career if you follow these very simple tasks.

Your greatest success will come when you can finally achieve momentum. Not only does it feel good, but it is productive, and gets you to the finish line quicker. But not all projects get there, and that is because clients aren't prepared. To get yourself prepared and into the momentum zone, follow these steps, in order.

1. Establish psychological safety
2. Cleanse the software vendor's database
3. Get your data ready before project kick-off
4. Bring design consultants into the project
5. Develop and test designs and extensions
6. Train users
7. Perform User Acceptance Training (UAT)
8. Go live

1. Establish psychological safety

Google has done extensive research and application on project teams to discover this key success factor: *teams* are more successful when psychological safety has been established.

So, what is this psychological safety?

Psychological safety is where any and all team members are heard and expected to be heard. As a matter of fact, they have to speak, each and every one of them. You could also call it a check-in process, or a safety net. Overall, the conclusion is that teams perform better when everyone is and expects to be heard. That doesn't mean 12 to 30 people sit in more and more meetings either. That would be counter-productive. It means, though, that everyone, at some point, is included and consulted.

Alternative organizational behavior approach

If you have read *Energy Trading and Risk Management,* you know I favor a certain leader and their style – they get the most out of your capability. That is: expecting people to be curious and think through issues. The type of person who discusses problems and provides alternatives to experiment with. Those whose experiments work often get to have more and more responsibility.

In meshing these two experiences, I suggest that if you create expectations that allow everyone to experiment, and you expect curiosity to solve problems, and you have the humility to discover the best outcomes, your teams will be successful. I prefer curiosity and experimentation – and reward those who perform this way – probably because I lived it and digested how it works. Folks worth millions driving around old beat up Jeep Cherokees bring humility, not attitudes. By the way, I drive a Ford F250, built to last a long time.

Unfortunately, the complete opposite of these two management approaches are applied when most projects start. They are off to the races to deliver more and more about less and less, to see who can create more perceptions than results. There is always pressure to deliver something now.

Some of the favorite project adjectives, for both consultants and clients alike:

- Bleeding the way
- Getting done before you start
- Show me how the system works on day one

For many, this is why turnover is rampant in commodity and energy trading, internally and

180

externally, on projects. Personally, if I write another line, I may turn to drinking, which I rarely do. Reality is that I am very, very calm at the beginning of a project. That's because I have a deliberate path. It's the end, or when I show up during a project that has little to no momentum, when I need a double martini – and I don't like martinis.

Creating a great start to a project is perceived as: having a great need to ramp up with a lot of resources quickly, getting them working together, and then all the forming, storming and norming phases work themselves out. In theory, I follow that. In practice, though, project turnover is so rampant that I suggest the opposite is how you will get project momentum.

Instead, clients have perceptions about who is the best consultant, and sales people claim that if you don't hire these consultants now, they are going to be taken by another project.

Please do not take this bait. These are deal-closing tactics to rush you to sign the software license, yet not any one of those people are available. The same six consultants, promised project after project, are working on four other projects, so there is little chance of getting them.

Instead of thinking there are 1 or 2 saviors, follow a disciplined approach and you won't need the best. You will need people who can follow your project management process. This process mitigates that talent issue I articulated earlier.

I would not allow one additional consultant who is not working on the next two project steps, to arrive until step three is complete. Again, I do not care what the software vendor or consulting firm is suggesting, or frightening you into. Let them go, trust me.

It doesn't matter how good your consultant is if you follow this approach.

2. Cleanse the software vendor's database

If you can find me one project that says they just took the vendor's "cleansed" – or "gold," "gold standard," "pristine," or whatever other adjective – database of referential data from customers to cash, and implemented the project without hiccups, I'll include in this book. Instead, scrambling around to cleanse it later is the major underlying reason projects go into reverse. Or if you can show me they don't still have a bunch of useless referential data cluttering their database, I will fly to your location and review it. And then I will post it on my website.

The database the vendor will send you is going to burn dollars as you chase, replace, and re-work. Many more hiccups will occur. Therefore, I suggest you completely wipe away 95% of the referential data immediately. Start fresh.

You may want to leave unit conversions, but even those are contentious at times. I mean wipe every counterparty, contract, price index, salutation, pipeline point, accounting chart, payment term, and trade type, among many others.

The only projects I have ever seen succeed had wiped the database spot clean, save just a few tables and data columns. No, the database is not "pristine", it is not "golden", it is not "cleansed", it is full of GIGO that will bite you very hard.

I have arrived on projects after kick-off, after they had already been going for three, four, and even twelve months, and it took me months to get control of the data migration along with the vendor's data. Many of my nights and weekends were wasted fixing these nightmares.

My nineteen-year-old, the kid who made a perfect score on the ACT, scoring as a college grad even before high school, with his borderline genius IQ, says to me, "Dad, you are a workaholic." My reply? "Thanks, I appreciate that." I took it as a compliment from a real overachiever.

However, I have been on projects where I have wiped the database clean, started from scratch and had counterparties, contracts, trades, logistics, and accounting codes from the client's account code structure, and have run the entire customer-to-cash process in two weeks to prove the database was working appropriately before putting in even more referential data. I recall how that was overlooked, but a key ingredient I am glad to have gained from their wares.

I have also seen projects with 12 consultants not do this basic step for months. Why? They are stumbling all over each other, experimenting with what they think is important. Even when someone supposedly had control of the database, regardless of the vendor or other consulting firm, I have seen so many missteps, poorly designed scripts migrating the wrong data. I have even seen someone leave old data in the database in a so-called "off" state, only to see it resurface when it was turned back on. Siggghhhhh.

3. Get your data ready before project kick-off

Referential data

Get your current data – referential data, not transactional data – in a state that is ready to load into the new system. It is no easy task.

In many cases, it takes months to get right. Plan on it.

The time really depends the state of your data and the size of your operation, though. A lot of over-promising and under-delivering of data migration happens on every project, which only delays it, one way or another.

Once you agree to getting your data ready, you also have to agree to *only* load the data that you currently use, not the wish list of data you think you might need.

I have seen a project go off the rails on price indexes alone, no pun intended. If you trade 100 different price indexes, and expect to trade many more in the future, that is great. I am glad you have vision and ability to grow. Projects do not have the luxury of chasing a dozen traders' dreams of what is possible. C/ETRM systems are not data warehouses for creating think-tanks based on some vision that has no merit.

Experimenting and running a think-tank are two different concepts.

Reality is that what you trade today is worth the dollars spent. Preparing for that AAA failure is not worth it and any project manager worth their weight in dollars, much less gold, should be able to keep control of scope creep and career-ending approaches.

There are untold projects where turnover is 80% and the consultants never see the end of a project. Projects can only chase what is in front of them and that is the reality you must enforce. Enforce is a strong word. We need to achieve the basics first, to ensure we start, and bring the design team to the project when they are really needed. This will leverage your dollars and ultimately lead to developing a great solution we are all happy with. And it starts with data.

Follow what I suggest and just load basic referential data first. Don't let anyone else on the project until you have control of the data.

I know many people who will argue against it, and say who cares about doing the basics well, just give me the tough solutions to solve and the rest will take care of itself. No. No, it won't and that is why some have more projects going off the rails than others.

I have seen reports that 25% of ETRM implementations are unsatisfactory, but how many people admit to poor stock trades? None, which is why I think 25% is low. There is no foolproof way to know, but I do know exactly what some firms' ratios are, and trust me, we need to talk.

Having the data is, therefore, really important.

Let's not forget, though, I expect that when I suggest the above, you have already defined every last report, in the front-, middle- and back-offices. If not, your chances for success drop substantially.

Transaction data

Trade migration is no small feat. I have seen promises of this taking a month, but realistically it takes months and months, and then more months to get done. I have seen the best stumble, believing they could achieve migration faster than expected. And when asked if it was done, they said yes – I cringed knowing it wasn't. We then end up keying or migrating more trades later. Eventually, if you are missing an entire class, or trade type, especially physical ones, design may not go as well as intended.

Processing some of these with alacrity, using proof-of-concept testing is highly recommended and will save time when the design and extensions are developed. This is especially so for those with more and more extensions being delivered. You can then isolate the problem quickly. Otherwise, your project could go into hyper mode and end up going backwards. Having to go back and discern that bad referential data, bad transactional data, or whether the code updates and/or extensions are the issue, create chaos – not agility.

I have seen 10-hour days turn into 18-hour days in a hurry, and projects literally end up going in reverse. Then, to mitigate going backwards they push the accelerator harder. But, if you push the accelerator while going backwards, you will only go backwards faster.

Try it in a parking lot sometime and you will feel what many project consultants have felt!

Guess what happens next. We do not adhere to step 1 of this process. I have seen people, both deserving and underserving, internally and externally, removed from a project.

Project turnover is up to 80% on many projects and most of those dollars are never seen again. Poof.

4. Bring design consultants into the project

Are we ready for the implementation consultants now?

If we have processed some transactions from customer-to-cash, and we did not get great big pop-ups or database crashes that destroyed all of the data, I think we are in a good place to bring on design consultants, internal and external.

We haven't discussed the number of design, test, sandboxes, etc. needed. The fewer the better is the best answer I can give you.

Seriously. I have seen where 42 people wanted a local copy of the software on their desktop to do their design tasks. That is not the best choice. The software vendor will send its entire support staff to support those 42 people who corrupt, disrupt and destroy each environment? Doubtful.

Depending on the size of your project, it is prudent to have 1-3 design environments, with a pristine or gold environment in which basic data, basic design and then code extensions are developed, tested and graduated.

In keeping the spirit of full disclosure. Let's not take the latest release as the best release from the software vendor either. Instead, let's start with their annual release, or the last patch or update. Over the course of the project, we may gravitate toward the annual release, but only after it has proven to be better than the previous version.

Stability is the basics I am suggesting, and suggesting heavily. And, praying, seriously. Basics are data, both referential and transactional, that accommodate the reporting needs. Knowing which reports we need, tells us what data we need, which drives the design process.

5. Develop and test designs and extensions

Hold your breath. Projects have to keep moving, so expect the consultants to know there are issues, that some of the code extensions, especially, are not ready to go. They will have known long before the original due dates, because their bosses are telling you it will be on time, and that the targets to deliver the extensions were "aggressive." Project pressures always exists. However, unrealistic expectations need to be discerned by the client. Too much pressure often brings more consultants, and more consultants bring more problems.

Therefore, if you know the user acceptance testing dates are at a risk, postpone them now.

The number of extensions on any project always ends in many more hours than ever planned. I have seen 200 hours turn into 3,000. I have seen projects scoped for 15,000 hours of programming end with over 35,000 hours.

There are certainly vendors touting they have one branch of code that everyone is on, regardless. There are cloud solutions to companies that are suggesting that these hours are not needed if you buy their software. All of this may be true.

How and why?

For numerous reasons, from the size of the trading operation, to their experience, to not having a budget beyond what they state. Leadership helps them ensure they provide their staff with an understanding that they do not want to spend the next 24-36 months on a project, so accept exactly how it works out-of-the-box. We will go from there.

This is rarely the path, though. Scoping extensions is very hard to do. In the requirements phase, you can't give enough information.

The other half is that many consultants do not understand trading, regardless of how long they have been around.

I wish there was a test for every consultant, proctored, to see who really knows trading and who doesn't. If you cannot connect the dots, you are going to see not just re-work, but work that should have been at the beginning, left until the end.

A quick example is where the accounting group had requested a short vs. long-term asset vs. liability report. It didn't get developed until the end. Then, when the programmer received it, it was full of complex rules. The company's policies and procedures were basically required to be included in the program. Again, accounting is not accounting. It is not in a perfect little box, fit for all.

It is rare that consultants know everything from book structure to balance sheets.

Developers and programmers certainly have not had much trading exposure, save the very narrow code they work in daily.

I have seen extensions where just mapping/interfacing one system to another was scheduled for 2-3 months, and 8 months later it was still an issue. From what I could see, which I already knew from working with them on other activities, was that neither the consultant, nor the developers knew anything of what was needed to achieve the solution. One promise after another, missed, broken and not delivered.

I have also worked on projects where we planned for over 20,000 hours of extensions, and the client took it down, for political and budget presentation, to a few thousand. This didn't serve them well, at all. It meant that the project, which was a phased approach, was not delivered in that approach and not in the original timelines. Over two years later – which meant millions more spent than originally budgeted – did it go live.

I have discovered a way to control extensions to ensure clarity at all stages. Naturally, for the price of this book, I am not going to divulge it here. When you hire **Front-2-Back**, you won't be disappointed with the approach and deliverables. It is truly game-changing.

6. Train users

This may seem counterintuitive. How can design take place if we don't know how to use the system? At the beginning of every project, the users are eager to see the system and get it up and running. When it is up and running, it is nearly perfectly predictable: watch them run!

All of a sudden, more and more meetings and other events, and the day-to-day job becomes an issue. Said another way, human nature has just taken over and everyone is hoping that someone else will pick up the project slack, and that the consultants will do it all. It happens this way. It never works well.

Therefore, when training is being done at project kick-off, another real awakening occurs on every project: it takes up to 6 weeks to just digest how to the system connects the dots. Hence, I suggest we connect the dots for you at **Front-2-Back**.

The project plan, though, has the initial design of 9 out of 11 major functional areas completed by the end of month two. But you don't even know how the system works, even at the 42,000-foot level. Half the consultants have no idea either. It's a mad rush, then, to slap something together to keep the project going in a timely manner. If you have done an ETRM project, you don't even want to continue reading any further, it brings up interesting experiences, to say the least. If you haven't worked a project, start reaching out to those who have. Ask someone who has, or call us at **Front-2-Back**. We will help you through the project planning so that your project starts well.

This is why I put user training up, right next to user acceptance testing. No doubt, for any project to be successful, employees will need to start learning the system at project kick-off. Invariably, I see a few people who take a project, not thinking of the future, but realize

197

after that it has propelled their career with promotions and pay raises. I know, I was in those shoes and I have watched others do it too!

Again, this one week of user training is not going to make everyone feel comfortable when UAT starts. You will still need people standing around who can guide you through the UAT. Do not be afraid to run right over to a consultant to ask questions. Until you are satisfied, keep going around and asking consultants.

At this point, you are not sure who has been doing what on the project. If you dive in and ask questions you will propel your UAT.

7. Perform User Acceptance Testing (UAT)

Ah, now the client gets into the system and starts testing away. Testing being taking the client data from a specific time – from the current or last few months – creating test scenarios and running those into the system with the basic, easier transactions up to the more complex in each iteration. Preparing for this stage is rarely done well. Consultants are constantly bird-dogging the client to develop test cases for months in advance of the UAT.

Months go by and little is ready. Too busy, not a problem today, and no doubt I understand that trading is moving twenty times faster than other business operations. Markets are changing rapidly, right in the middle of projects, with new products and new counterparties, you are not sure where to begin.

Begin with the transactions you do the most. Get real, live data, and test it.

The secret is that if you do not document, and I mean screen shots and/or printing the reports, when it comes to go-live and something doesn't work in your area, you have nothing to prove your testing was done well.

You may have tested it like no other. You may have added additional scenarios above and beyond. I see this often. At go-live, a new version, a new extension, or what I like to call "gremlins" have changed the code and all of the testing you have done suddenly no longer works.

Consultants also know you do not test things thoroughly, and even if pressed, some will not test the system.

I too have had the most politically correct, smartest people come up to me and say, since you did this I don't need to test this, right? I pull them aside and say, the minute I leave, something will break. I am testing and putting everything I can on your SharePoint for you to use as a training guide and to ensure everything I worked on works, and was proven to work. But, it is still up to you to test your system.

I have had clients, even just one year later, all of sudden have a software application stop working in some form or fashion. And often, they are not sure if it really ever worked. I have asked, since I am not going to keep your testing on my computer, for confidentiality and ethics, will you pull up your SharePoint and search your records. The response, "well, we needed space and the SharePoint system was deleted." My thought, not response: sighhhhh.

These things happen often and without proper test procedures and documentation, you have little to fall back on in proving to yourself, much less the rest, that you did a thorough job.

Some, I know, never tested a thing. They just hoped the functionality was there, or that if it wasn't, they just report a bug to the vendor after go-live. Many consultants, including myself, have left a project knowing certain areas were just not tested well. That is unfortunate, but we can't make you test it.

8. Go live

I have seen some projects go live well, and I have seen some not work for another six months.

There is certainly going to be something that is not complete, and everyone knows it, but you have to move forward and go live. You can run a parallel or you can cutover and start moving forward.

I make no recommendation here. It is client specific to discern which approach will be acceptable and which is preferred. It depends on many factors, so use your own judgment for that.

Certainly, parallel seems safer but for some that may not be possible due to the number of hours in a day, or the number of trades they make each day.

If you opt for a cut-over, I would expect that this is the first time I would allow the term Triple-A. Triple-A to the extent of what can, realistically, be delivered. You will know immediately whether the functionality – that does have some form of any, all and/or automatically – works as expected when a trader doesn't scream. Everything should be good for the current and forward positions and valuation. If two months later it is discovered a position was significantly off in volume or value, that is the trader's issue.

For accounting, compare the balance sheet accounts down to subledgers for any material changes after cutover. This includes income statements too. The balance sheet side, especially if the market has not moved, shouldn't move much either. If in the first month you have major market moves, which I have often seen, there is no doubt the balance sheet will have changed from the short-term vs. the long-term for both assets and liabilities. I had this happen early in my career, and we were scratching our heads. After studying the changes in the forward curve, from the prior month-end, it all made sense.

Therefore, having everyone do a little extra due diligence when going live, and doing it for several months is key. I don't mean an extra 4 hours a day, but at least spot check the bigger items and have someone analyze the details in a few areas that are key to your income and balance sheet accounts.

I don't have to say anything to the risk folks. Why? Trust me, they will tell you!

For more information of how **Front-2-Back** Consulting can serve you, and for some bonus information and downloads, visit: www.frontmidback.com/book-bonus

Chapter 16: Post Project Assessment: Benefit Analysis

Mr. Berley, you have lost it. I have spent months, even years on this project and you want me to assess the benefits as compared to our original goals?

Yep!

Why?

Two months after a project kick-off, the project goals have long been forgotten. Focus turns to any number of tangents. However, anything we do, if we can't measure it, we shouldn't be doing it.

Measure the project benefits. There will, of course, be some that were missed, but others, who didn't expect it in the back-office who have had ah-ha moments, will be elated.

I would suggest starting with a survey, at a high level, to everyone through a third-party survey service, like Google Forms or Survey

Monkey. Start with general questions, and then ask for open-ended input. Make it mandatory to add input and see what the outcomes are at the high levels of the front-, mid- and back-office process. I would then follow-up with another survey six months after go-live, and another after one year.

You will want to hear about what everyone likes, but know that there will also be areas that were not well designed, so they aren't used well. There will be a lot of opportunity to clean up and fix issues. Be prepared for this follow-up, expect it, plan for it, and budget for it. Slacking on this step would be like your engineering department, who just built a brand-new plant, saying "Ah, since it is new plant we don't need to monitor, test or do any maintenance for years."

Way too much time, energy, money and pride has gone into your project. Follow-up and bring in others to provide insight.

For more information of how **Front-2-Back** Consulting can serve you, and for some bonus information and downloads, visit: www.frontmidback.com/book-bonus

Chapter 17: Upgrading your C/ETRM System

Don't Upgrade your ETRM System!

Why?

Has anyone articulated the benefits of why this is important?

Is someone suggesting your version and/or releases are so old you have to upgrade?

Has anyone truly understood the problems you face?

Has anyone communicated the opportunity cost you face from the undiscovered firepower of current versions?

Has any consultant ever connected the dots front, middle and back, in your ETRM system with real energy trading, risk management and accounting experts?

Has any consultant brought direct experience as a trading leader, risk director, controller, and consultant to your doorstep to understand all the above for you and your company?

We propose two upgrade alternatives:

1. Bring in big consulting firms, issue 6 security badges, clear out a conference room for months, receive 25,000-foot process diagrams, neatly placed into the SharePoint system nobody looks at, and which IT will delete in a year because they need the space. Then, for another $1-2 million, maybe get some deliverables.
2. Use **Front-2-Back**, who provides one point of contact who has actually worked in the back-office, mid-office, front-office, and consulted on countless ETRM system projects. Someone who can quickly discern your problems and opportunity costs, and who can propose relevant solutions, and then connect the DOTS by Doing One Thing Smarter and delivering real benefits.

For more information of how **Front-2-Back** Consulting can serve you, and for some bonus information and downloads, visit:
www.frontmidback.com/book-bonus

Chapter 18: Switching ETRM Systems

There are systems that are much harder than others to use, much less implement. They cost way too much to maintain. A million dollars to upgrade a few components, and several million to bring it up-to-date.

We are actually seeing several companies switch from certain vendors because systems are too complex, and there have been too many broken promises. Enough is enough.

In the long term, there are vendors I would switch you to today! They may not have everything you need – nobody does – but they will eventually!

There are a few systems that were poorly implemented and it will take millions to fix those as well. It's easier, in many cases, to start over.

The best advice, is to always keep your options open!

For more information of how **Front-2-Back** Consulting can serve you, and for some bonus information and downloads, visit:

www.frontmidback.com/book-bonus

Chapter 19: Key C/ETRM Success Factors

I would like to provide a summary of the critical areas and path that we suggest you may want to follow to ensure you have a successful C/ETRM system process, from selection to implementation and for future use.

Why are you buying a C/ETRM system? It is often sold as the front-office capability and needs because they make the money and have the influence in the selection process. Often, however, the greatest beneficiaries are the middle- and back-offices. If you include them early, the benefits will increase. The data and information needed, as data grows larger and larger, makes the entire process more efficient and effective.

The main concept is that no project can go well if we do not know the information we must have out of the system. That means we need to know the reports – the reports from front-2-back.

In knowing the reports, you will be able to determine the data attributes you'll need. When C/ETRM systems come with over 10,000 data attributes, it may seem daunting. It is especially daunting six months into a project, if reporting needs and, subsequently, data needs start surfacing and sending projects backwards. "Burning dollars" is a huge issue when it comes to reporting. It is as nearly as predictable as the setting of the sun.

In preparing for purchasing a new system, the scope and requirements are a tricky part of the project. You can't really get into the how and why for each requirement, but you do have define what is in scope, and which requirements are really must-have, nice-to-have, or not required.

Once you have selected a software vendor, planning and execution are key. I have provided thoughts to help you achieve project success with the cost/benefit analysis of how to stage your process, from data migration, to consultants, to completing the project with optimal outcomes. No two project are alike. Not even at the same company.

For the future, I believe we will have a breakthrough and maturity in this space, where Big Data, – which provides tremendous insights and uses 21st-century valuation techniques – along with consolidation in this space will move us closer to a truly one-software-vendor solution.

As in my last book, I save the best for last.

Human nature ensures we are going to have contentious and challenging projects. All leaders need to know, expect, and plan for it. Leaders need to engage in the project, literally stopping by the project team ad-hoc, and into meetings to see how the project is progressing. Leaders, not just the project leaders, need to learn the names of consultants and engage them as if they were employees.

It is the only way to make a project consultant work further to help you achieve success. Going to lunch with many, and often, is going to give you real insight into the project. Making everyone a team member and stating so to everyone before a project is even in the selection phase, and reiterating it throughout the project through your action and presence, will allow you to see much greater success. You will truly know if you truly have the ultimate goal: Project Momentum.

For more information of how **Front-2-Back** Consulting can serve you, and for some bonus information and downloads, visit: www.frontmidback.com/book-bonus